Stefanie Honold

PINK:CODE

The 8 keys
to unlocking the secret
of unlimited success
in network marketing

Bibliographic information of the German National Library:
The German National Library lists this publication in the
German National Biography: detailed bibliographic data is
available on the Internet via: http://dnb.d-nb.de

Cover- and image design: Agentur DESIGNUM,
www.DESIGNUM.de
Cover based on an idea by Jörn Degenhard

Photography: Lukas /lukasleertaste.de

ISBN: 9783758303661

© 2023 Stefanie Honold
Production and publishing: BoD - Books on Demand, Norderstedt

PINK:CODE

CONTENTS

Preface — Seite 6

On the still unknown path to oneself — Seite 13
1st Key: PINK — Seite 22
1. Ease & fun — Seite 25
2. Think big - without thinking at all — Seite 29
3. Reflection & intuition — Seite 32
4. Learn to unlearn & be brave — Seite 35

More freedom and standing up for yourself — Seite 43
2nd Key: POSITIVE — Seite 52
1. The art of indulging — Seite 55
2. Expect nothing, give everything — Seite 60
3. Start today, rather than tomorrow — Seite 62
4. The art of constantly thinking positively — Seite 66

Self-liberation - the breakthrough to a new life — Seite 71
3rd Key: PERSONALITY — Seite 78
1. Mindset – tweaking your own perspective — Seite 81
2. Humility and gratitude — Seite 85
3. Change and personality development — Seite 90
4. The next level: Be your own brand — Seite 93

One system makes it possible — Seite 99
4th Key: PROMOTION — Seite 108
1. Action – become visible and make it happen — Seite 111

2. Communication – a core element in pink	Seite 115
3. Unique authenticity	Seite 118
4. Recognition is valuable	Seite 121
New thinking, new luck	Seite 129
5th Key: POWER	Seite 138
1. The value of reliability	Seite 141
2. Trust is unique	Seite 145
3. That little bit more: Commitment	Seite 149
4. Teambuilding: Expansion & Consolidation	Seite 153
From idea consume6th Key: PLAN	Seite 161
6. Schlüssel: PLAN	Seite 174
1. Having a vision – defining and knowing why	Seite 178
2. Focus and goal orientation	Seite 181
3. Structured – being active with a system	Seite 184
4. "Double CC" – Consistency and continuity	Seite 188
Leading with heart means, becoming more pink	Seite 195
7th Key: PARTNERSHIP	Seite 202
1. Does it fit or not?	Seite 205
2. Reciprocity on equal footing	Seite 208
3. Recognizing potential	Seite 212
4. Be the best version of yourself	Seite 215
S for Start - the only way to reach your goal	Seite 223
8th Key: PASSION	Seite 232
1. Commitment to yourself	Seite 235
2. The pinnacle: Level of passion	Seite 240

THE PINK:CODE.
A WAY TOWARDS PASSION.

To my
fantastic team

PREFACE

Imagine you're working hard and dedicated, but you don't even realize it. Because you enjoy it. Because it doesn't burden you. Because it doesn't feel like work at all. And because what you do even fills you up inside and gives you a certain joyful satisfaction. Almost like a cherished hobby.

You are convinced that such thing doesn't exist? But how can it be, that supposedly extremely successful people in particular, claim that they have never really worked in their lives? Rather, they have turned their hobby into their profession, or they are so fulfilled by their tasks that they don't even consider it work per se. Are they all overachievers? Dreamers? Fantasists detached from reality? Or even reality deniers who are only permanently deluding themselves? People who talk themselves into believing anything? No, probably not. Quite the opposite. Women and men who claim that they have never really worked, are downright fulfilled. They have hit the bull's eye in their professional work and activities almost as if they had aimed at an imaginary target with "my good life" at its center. The word "fulfilled" has therefore been used quite deliberately in this context, because they are "fulfilled" by their activities, by their personal drive, by their goals and by their own creative power. Their activities fill them up! What unites these committed individuals is a single word: Passion!

It is an intense passion, an inner dedication to something that satisfies a person so much that they are almost infused with it and because of this, the activity has turned into a positive automatism. Conscious becomes unconscious – you just do it. Without specifically thinking about it, without having concrete intentions, without planning and without weighing up the pros and cons. There is also no compulsion, no real obligation and certainly no cognitive feeling of I "must." You do it because it is "right", because you are positively convinced of it and because it has proven to be useful for a certain purpose time and time again. Perhaps, also because it simply gives you pleasure and this in the most diverse, manifold way. It serves a higher purpose, perhaps even a personal advantage. And precisely because you do it over and over again, execute it, start it, do it, or apply it, this particular action becomes second nature. An automatism develops, which is to your own advantage - in whatever form. So much so, that you no longer think about it, but has rather eliminated the deliberate intention. It is like brushing your teeth – simply doing it without thinking about it. It is an internalized automatism. Would we call this active work? Probably not. A must? A personal compulsion? Something that weighs you down, where you have to fight with yourself? Something you have to overcome and mentally torture yourself over? No way, brushing teeth is an automatism that you don't have to force yourself to do, even though it is not a reflex. No one walks past the bathroom and reflexively reaches for a toothbrush. What a grotesque idea.

But why is brushing one's teeth so normal and yet such a self-evident process that it has turned into an automatic routine for us? Because everyone just knows what the benefits are. Healthy teeth mean a reduced risk of being tormented by toothache and less frequent visits to the often-feared dentist. In addition, there is improved dental hygiene, which benefits both you and the people around you. Brushing your teeth only comes with advantages. We do it simply because it benefits us.

But can this possibly also apply in terms of active work? You bet it can! This advantageous effect is noticeably achieved when effort, commitment and return are worthwhile and when the general conditions, the so-called contextual factors, also have a correspondingly positive effect.

Let's consider a concrete example to illustrate this further: An employed geriatric nurse gets up at 6 a.m. every morning. She has breakfast and then takes the crowded bus to work. Unfortunately, she doesn't have a seat - again. Hence, she ends up standing in an overcrowded bus. As you can imagine, the day is already off to a good start. Her nerves are put to the test right at the beginning of the day. When she arrives at work, she already knows that a hectic, stressful, and demanding eight-hour day will be waiting for her – and the prevailing staff shortage is just the cherry on top. Also, as it happens, her shift supervisor is not exactly the incarnation of friendliness or good humor. Instead of the occasional praise, "Thanks, you did a good job!" she usually gets a "Can you go a little faster?" As much as she appreciates her job, the tasks it entails and feels personally committed to it, the circumstances described above do not give rise to any fulfilling joy. Will this employee, after 35 or 40 years in the industry, who feels like she has worked herself to death, rave about how wonderful her working life was?

Hardly! Will she say, "It feels like I've never really worked a day in my life!" Certainly not. Especially when she sees her modest paycheck month after month, because she will know well that her tremendous effort, her great, even magnificent commitment has not resulted in any noticeable (financial) advantage for her. The effort has not really paid off in terms of numbers. A look at her bank account, including all government deductions, will probably evoke a negative feeling in her – despair, incompleteness, or rumination. Mental stress! How is a positive automatism supposed to be initiated in these dire circumstances? An automatism that would allow her to internalize her effort in such a way that she no longer feels it or perceives it as such? Impossible!

On the other hand, let's consider the quite contrary example of a dedicated, motivated member of the network marketing industry. Everything she does, all her activities, benefit her and the wider organization team. Making new contacts, cultivating relationships, sponsoring, on-boarding new hires, preparing training and meetings, and pushing further sales activities – all of this will take up the said networker's time almost around the clock. It is a role that is very intense, demanding and requires responsibility and ownership of tasks at the highest level. It is a constant feeling and inner state of action, commitment, intrinsic motivation, and continuous energy. But at the same time, it is a commitment that pays off. Network professionals invest themselves in their team members and will give everything for them. Why? Because it fills them with joy and happiness, when it is up to them to make their partners more successful than they could have ever imagined. But don't get me wrong, this is not an act of pure philanthropy. Rather, the whole system of network marketing is designed to challenge others, and in doing so, to make them successful. Because this is the only way to achieve your own desires, clearly defined success and to reach the appropriate heights enabling your visions to come true. Everything you invest comes back in a different way, almost like the law of nature. Once you have experienced this, you will understand how this feeling makes you happy, drives you and boosts your own performance to new levels. It's fulfilling. So much so, that these activities become more and more internalized and automated. To the point where you just do it and at the same time it no longer feels like work, but rather a blessing to do both for yourself and for others. Because the benefits that are generated from it are indescribably great, highly valuable, and conducive to one's own goals. In the end, there is only one decisive question: How do you manage to reach this stage? In fact, the crucial word here is the "how."

This book that you're holding in your hands is meant to demonstrate exactly that. It's not another praise song for the network marketing system. Instead, the focus is on answering the question of "how." After all, what is the benefit of merely repeating the long known infamous wisdom of: "You have to get out of your comfort zone!" Of course, this exhortation is generally true, but you probably already know that yourself. The question that still remains however is: HOW do you do it? What do you have to do to put this wise advice into practice? How can you motivate yourself to go the extra mile? And how do you succeed in the end so that you don't get stuck in your comfort zone? Or put differently: What does it take for you to leave your previous zone of comfort and transition into a new zone of need fulfilment or "flow?" A set of demanding tasks where you are convinced that they benefit you in such a way that the activities associated with them become more and more automatic. And all of a sudden, it's no longer the negative effort that counts but the positive return from it. Of course, this is a question of mindset. It is the consideration of a two-sided coin. It's just a matter of focusing supposedly on the right page.

Because suddenly life, your job, the daily success-promoting, individual measures become more **colorful, more exciting, brighter, more luminous, more cheerful, plumper, more intense**, maybe even **shim-**

mer more, are **more joyful, sweet, charming, hopeful, reassuring, positive** and **emotional**, but also **more self-confiden**t. And do you know what else all these adjectives describe? A very specific color and it's called "pink!" It's not for nothing that they say "One sees through rose-colored glasses", which means something like: To have a positive view on something. Whoever thinks, acts, or lives like that, whose mindset is truly shifted towards "pink", doesn't work anymore. These will be the people that do something because they love it, because it fulfills them, because it makes them happy and because the activities have automatically become second nature to them. Do you know what I call that? Someone who is in the middle of the **Pink:Code!**

On the still unknown path to oneself

All roads lead to Rome - a common saying that is often used to refer to the many ways of achieving a goal. The origin of this saying dates back to 20 B.C. At that time, the Roman Emperor Augustus had all the capitals of the provinces within the Roman Empire engraved on a magnificent column. In the middle however, there was only one name: Rome - and the distances to the respective cities in question. This was not only to document the enormous dimensions of the empire at that time, but also to emphasize that Rome would always be the center of the world. Because no matter where you come from – all roads will eventually lead to Rome!

A nice saying that somehow fits me and my life like no other. I too, have taken many detours to finally end up where I am today: At the top! No, I surely did not take the direct route. It was not a straight line, the picture-perfect CV, with the starting point leading directly to the goal. Why not? To be frank, for many different reasons. On the one hand, I didn't even know my current goal at the beginning. So, I couldn't get there, let alone take the most direct path. On the other hand, this path that I have traveled until the beginning of my successful network marketing life today has led me through so many stages with so many learning experiences. Every experience, every learning, every new insight was at the same time a little nudge that changed my direction. In this way, I came a little closer, in incremental steps to where I am today in a rather unconscious way. For me, this meant evolving from the picturesque Lake Constance in Switzerland, out into the big wide world – step by step, until I finally reached today's "Pink Paradise." The Pink:Code itself was always there – first rather unconsciously, then more consciously and finally with full intention moving towards my personal passion and the key to success.

If I had known more about the Pink:Code as a child or had consciously aligned my actions with it in my youth, who knows whether my life would have turned out very differently. Maybe, maybe not- I really don't know. What is important, is that I now know the meaning of this special and extraordinary attitude towards life, that I have internalized it and can clearly and intentionally draw benefit from it. In fact, it is so crucial for many other things in life, that I decided to tell you about it and to share all of it with you in these upcoming pages. Because clearly, the Pink:Code has something for everyone. In its essence, it is a unique, lively and real-life philosophy that can give everyone a bit of support, security, confidence, self-esteem and joy in his or her life. It does so by triggering a permanently positive mindset. Once you have discovered it, you will probably never turn away from it again, because the Pink:Code is real and also supportive, encouraging, applicable and ready to be integrated into your life as well! The reason? Quite easy: To think positively, to live positively and to act positively is just simply pleasant. It feels good, you feel comfortable and breathe a little more easily, you can live more intensely and always start the day with joy. This mindset brings light into every life, into every daily routine and accompanies one in the completion of daily tasks and challenges. It lifts you up, instead of pulling you down like a heavy anchor. And no, someone who lives and breathes the Pink:Code is not a daydreamer or someone who strolls through life out of touch with reality. Not at all. Unpleasant things, negative events, sorrows and fears - all this remains just as much a part of real life, but what is important, is the question of how one deals with such unpleasant, sometimes stressful situations. How do I assess such events? From which angle do I view them and, above all, what conclusions and lessons can I draw from them? This is exactly where positive thinking begins in the first place. This is where the Pink:Code really comes into its own.

As unoriginal as the comparison may seem, the following expression is and remains important and correct: Is a glass of water half full or half empty? We observe the same actual state but with two completely different ways of looking at it. One negative and one positive. The way I perceive reality to be, also depends exclusively on me and my corresponding mindset. It defines my way of looking at things. If the glass of water is half empty for me, then this can imply the following hypothetically: I must be constantly thirsty. I must limit my drinking. But if I am feeling thirsty, I must drink only a little water, because otherwise there will be nothing left. I'm soon threatened with scarcity... Clearly, a negative way of thinking leads to constantly ruminating on the "what if…?" A mindset that eventually pulls me deeper and deeper into a negative, threatening emotional vortex. Fears of loss, worry, resignation, and constant concerns about the resulting consequences. A dark, gloomy mood manifests itself more and more.

However, if one regards the glass of water as half full, a completely different emotionality is being promoted. Eventually, my thoughts are triggered to become much more positive and motivated by nature: I still have enough water. That gives me strength. Nothing can happen to me, I am safe. The amount is enough – even if I get extremely thirsty. I could even give some of the water to others. And even if I take a sip or two, I still have enough left. Neither fear of loss, nor threatening images or situations come to mind. Quite the opposite. The view of the glass half full does not allow for any negative thoughts at all. Confidence determines my attitude and positive perspectives encourage me, motivate me, and give me new strength.

All of this is despite the initial situation being absolutely the same: A half-filled glass of water. Do you notice how much your way of thinking, your way of cognitively evaluating something, influences you and your emotions? You alone have the choice. If the world is gray and gloomy for you - then the glass is also half empty. Or is it half full for you? If so, then positive, motivating, and inspiring thoughts will surround you. This has nothing to do with artificially glossing over problems. You just evaluate a circumstance from a different point of view and draw different conclusions accordingly. You see the world in a solution-oriented way, instead of resignedly through rose-colored glasses. Welcome to the Pink:Code!

Honestly, this color speaks for itself. It is warm, friendly, cheerful, striking, even entertaining, and stimulating. It's no wonder that I've never seen people in positions of power or regulatory decision-makers in politics or business dressed in pink. After all, it's not known to be all too cheerful there. Just the idea of seeing a head of government styled completely in pink - wonderful, spectacular, slightly bizarre, but probably also completely utopian. The network marketing industry on the other hand, is refreshingly different. Impressive personalities, all the way to top executives, will have deliberately developed a strong liking for the color pink and probably left a striking impression by doing so. In fact, they all know why; because they can and because they are women and men who have accomplished something in their lives. Not "whippersnappers" but high achievers! Constantly overachieving because they think positively because they are internally adjusted and calibrated "pink." They are all people who positively influence others to unlock greatness of all kinds! And who - whether consciously or unconsciously - have internalized the Pink:Code, live it, turn it into reality and at the same time exemplify it.

I am happy that my life is so pink today - through and through! But it didn't start out all too pink for me. When I first saw the light of day in a small-town right-on Lake Constance, I literally had the umbilical cord wrapped around my neck. A life-threatening situation! Danger looming on every front. It may be that this dangerous circumstance alone, ensured that I was a real fighter from the very beginning, and have remained one to this day. In any case, it was a unique start to life that somehow left its mark on me. Although I was later able to benefit from some pleasant circumstances in life, I can say with full conviction that nothing was ever handed to me on a silver platter. Where I am today and what I am today is the final product of honest work, a lot of diligence, sweaty effort, accepting and overcoming challenges, conscious commitment, a will of iron and a lot of Pink:Code. Because this said work and the fulfillment of tasks, can only be accomplished with a correspondingly positive attitude. A clear commitment to life, to experience, to personal success and the associated enjoyment of freedom is the quintessence of true passion. And how that works, is exactly what I want to show you in this book.

Born in Constance, raised in Radolfzell, twenty kilometers away - that's how one would put it in the typical accuracy of a true German. In the middle of the idyll and on the shores of Lake Constance. Couldn't be any better, could it? Although I went to school in my hometown and attended the humanist grammar school there until the 10th grade, I still felt like I was always on vacation at the lake. Not because I was constantly skipping classes, but rather because I had the great fortune to be allowed to live at my grandparents' campsite, which they managed on the Mettnau peninsula of Lake Constance. The season always ran from May to October - exactly the time when I could be seen frolicking among tents and caravans. What a sense of freedom! Sounds like a hell of a lot of fun, and it was, but from my early childhood, life also included work. It was my constant companion. And so, I became aware very early on, that nothing in life is ever for free. Especially not success! In fact, freedom is always closely linked to the topics of work, commitment, and goals – one cannot be without the other and as you will soon learn and read, my experiences in the course of life have confirmed and clarified this to me again and again.

Can you imagine what this beautiful atmosphere at the lakeside does to you? The environment is surely a paradise for children. In the middle of nature, right on the shore of the lake, lots of sunshine and fresh air, but - and this is crucial - around me there was always a good mood and cheerfulness as well. Certainly, because the people who came to our campsite were in an all-round holiday mood. And what is the mood like on vacation? The best mood possible! Bright faces, laughter, and friendliness were all around me, wherever I looked and to whomever I spoke to. Something like that, definitely leaves a mark. Does it come by any surprise then, that I am quite the positive spirit myself? Certainly not. Now, I am well aware that not everyone is lucky enough to grow up in such an environment, but all the clearer is the message I have for you in this context: Try to create a positive environment for yourself! I bet that the next question that will run through your minds is: "Easy to say - but how?"

I CREATE A POSITIVE ENVIRONMENT FOR MYSELF, BY...

1. ... no longer letting myself be dragged down by negative news in the media. How? By not consuming it at all.
2. ... surrounding myself exclusively with positive-minded people.
3. ... consistently refraining from negative conversations of any kind.
4. ... surrounding myself with positive things and putting myself in a good mood. This is helped, among other things, by wearing light-co lored clothes instead of dark ones, listening to upbeat music instead of sad, slow music, and getting enough exercise every day. A thirty-minute walk is enough.
5. ... telling myself in front of the mirror in the morning why I like my self, what I can do, and what I will accomplish today.
6. ... rewarding myself every day for something I have achieved, no matter what! Because I deserve it!

The "work" I just mentioned happened almost playfully on the side. In the morning for example, I sold the breakfast-rolls at the campsite. My grandmother gave me a small pad and a pencil and showed me how to add up the prices for the rolls. Great, so I could do math before I even went to school and who knows, maybe that early "sales experience" has something to do with how I ended up in referral marketing today.

For me, the campground was something like what other children knew as "playing shop." Only mine was bigger and more lifelike, but I also earned my first very small amounts of pocket money here. I collected beautiful stones from the shore, painted them, and put them in a box. It was my personal treasure chest. I then moved on to find a great spot where many of our guests had to pass by again and again, and then sold the colorfully painted stones to our campers as souvenirs. Can you get your first direct selling experience any earlier? I don't think so and since the reactions of "my customers" were all consistently good, nice, friendly and thus positive, I have to this day an absolutely positive attitude toward the subject of "distribution and sales."

Yes, those were easy times that I got to enjoy. In that, they were almost taken for granted and yet they also had a catch, one that I always recognized when the six weeks of summer vacation were over. It was about that time when all the children returned to school and guess what the first thing was that they talked to each other about? Exactly, about their vacations, about the trips they took with their parents and what they had experienced in the past weeks, in Italy, Spain, or France. Only I had the same answer year after year when they asked me where I had spent my time off: "I was at home!" Because we were never away during the summer vacations. How could we? During that time, it was the pivotal high season at the campground – our business. It was the busy season and the time of the year where my family earned the most income. Therefore, there was no time or intent of traveling at all and to add right away, I didn't miss it either. Not at all, in fact it was a lot of fun to be part of the business I called home. The campground was about ten minutes away from my parents' apartment and as early as May, I moved in with my grandmother in a fantastically large camping trailer with a bunk bed, where I was always allowed to sleep on top. A dream for any child - and even more so for me. From there I commuted to school because the route was not really very different or longer. At noon I came back, did my homework - mostly while sitting in the sun - and afterwards I was allowed to enjoy a bit of freedom, to romp, to play, but also to help grandma. Sometimes in the kiosk, sometimes at the reception - there was always a lot to do, and I was assigned appropriate tasks, which I also completed with pride and joy. But I didn't see this as work on my part, but rather as fun. That's why, even as a child, I experienced the so-called "optimization of the workplace" that we always like to talk about today. True to the motto: Work where you want, when you want and with whom you want! In this respect, I experienced and enjoyed a permanent holiday feeling, despite all the work and tasks I had to do. Today, looking back, I can say that while other children had six weeks of summer vacation during school, I had five to six months of vacation - during which I also happened to have school.

1st Key: **PINK**

Colors are not only beautiful to look at nor are they only unique by nature or merely there to bring visual variety into our lives. Rather, every color stands for something specific. It expresses something, symbolizes emotions, reflects moods, and paints a very unique picture of reality. It is a question of type, character and attitude towards life which is commonly expressed in the colors your wear and when. Do you know that distinct feeling of when you visit someone for the first time in a foreign apartment or house? You enter and almost involuntarily let everything sink in. But what makes an impression? What forms the first impression? What sticks in your mind? The type, shape and design of the furniture? The themes of the pictures? How tidy it is – or not? No, psychology gives very precise answers to this. For one thing, you first notice the individual scent that lingers in the rooms, because everyone, without exception, within their four walls, has their very own delicate, personal scent. The most striking thing however, is the impression of the color palette. We immediately recognize which colors dominate in each of the respective rooms. At first glance, it's not a matter of red, green or blue, but we first notice the degree of brightness that catches our eye in the new surroundings. We automatically distinguish between light and dark, between more white or more black. It is neither a valuation nor evaluation. It's an emotional response rather than a rational one. Also, because one involuntarily tries to classify the new. One wants to categorize, to find one's way emotionally. Have you ever experienced this yourself? You look around, wanting to know where you are and who you are dealing with. It is because your inner voice tells you that the "color world" in which someone primarily resides, says a lot about them and only when you have decided about the shade - namely light or dark - can you go a little deeper, bit by bit into details. Because then you start to look for more specific variations in color. Why? Because they also speak for themselves and have a fundamental expressiveness about someone else.

You know what it's like when someone comes along like a "colorful bird" with bright feathers? Someone like that, stands out, is dazzling, probably also quite self-confident and seems to be what you might call a "show off." Others, on the other hand, are more the simple, elegant, lighter type. Such a person prefers white, beige, sandy colors or at most very light pastel shades. A color palette that quickly puts someone like this in the "spotlight." People who stand for these shades are surrounded by the aura of lightness. This look is friendly, cosmopolitan, gentle and tender. Colors of this shade literally float, supporting spring and summer feelings. And then there is the dark corner - black, anthracite, gray, navy blue, dark brown. All colors that absorb light, seem heavy and sometimes even oppressive or depressive. And now imagine you're entering a house for the first time and it's decorated in white through and through. At most a few splashes of color here and there, but otherwise white dominates. No question: You will quickly open up, feel comfortable, move freely. The friendly atmosphere will envelop you, will carry you. In addition, the illumination in these rooms simply radiates a comfortable feel-good vibe. Brightness gives light instead of soaking it up. Add to that a little sunshine and these spaces are flooded with a palpable positivity. If, on the other hand, you were to stay in a dark to black environment, all your feelings and your impressions would almost be reversed. Right? I have nothing against black - this darkness also exudes a certain elegance due to the mysticism it contains, but lightness and positivity? No, not really. So, ask yourself, what do you associate with the striking, cheerful color pink? More light or dark impressions and sensations? Rather a good mood and positive mood? Or would pink perhaps even depress you? Probably not. After all, doesn't a sad person usually talk about having dark, gloomy thoughts? How nice would it be if such a person could laugh and finally shout: "Yes, I see a bright future, a future in pink!" - that would be a statement with weight, wouldn't it? But that's exactly what it's all about: Seeing pink by thinking pink and acting pink.

That's exactly what the Pink:Code is to a certain extent. A certain way of thinking combined with a positive way of starting and living – each and every day. Day by day and thus for every year of your life. Imagine how much easier, more pleasant, and solution-oriented your mindset would become if you could face every new challenge with a smile. That is, when you are "pink-oriented." How do you do that? Certainly not in a heartbeat. If you're not already "pink minded" in your head, you'll have to prepare first. Meaning, first entering the jungle of negative thoughts, out of a dark, pessimistic world and into the brightness. But on this point too, I will gladly answer the question of "how" instead of just leaving you alone with the mere invitation, to just step into the light. An effective method for getting better at facing a problem in pink, little by little, works as follows: Preferably, stand in front of a mirror. Look at yourself. Look closely. What is your posture like? Are you standing straight with your head held up high? Or do you have more of a submissive, slightly pre-resigned posture with slumped shoulders and a slightly lowered head? Attention! It all starts with the right posture. Put your hands on your hips. Stand up straight, and stretch slightly. Chest out - yes, men as well as women - and then raise your head slightly, so that the chin protrudes almost a bit provocatively. Great, with this posture you are already fully poised for victory and thus in pink mode! What follows now is by no means silly, but important: Tell your reflection in the mirror about the challenge you face and that you want to tackle today. Ha, with this posture you are as strong as a rock. This problem is not a challenge that can make you cave in, is it? So then go ahead and confirm it, say the solution out loud, right to your own face in the mirror. What are you going to do to meet the challenge? Say it, smile at the same time - and now you are in the middle of the Pink:Code.

THE FOUR MOST IMPORTANT FEATURES, THAT CHARACTERIZE THE KEY: **PINK**

1. EASE AND FUN

Did you know that making a serious face requires about five times more muscles of your face down to your stomach than making a friendly face with a smile? That fact alone speaks for itself. It makes you wonder why so many people go through everyday life with an almost entirely grumpy face. Maybe they should take a look at the famous quote by the great Charlie Chaplin, who once said: "A day without laughter is a day wasted!" He's right. For me, this is a clear indication that the famous comedian already had a "pretty pink" attitude about a hundred years ago.

Network marketing is a business that makes fun the priority. No nonsense, no shenanigans, but instead a joyful business that is conducted with all seriousness. This does not have to be a contradiction! If you have fun doing what you do, you do it with a certain lightness at the same time. Both go hand in hand with single-mindedness and determination. That's exactly how the network business works. Despite all the fun, you are still focused and do the best you can. But why is having fun so important? And what is essentially pink about it anyway? And - can work really be fun? A crucial factor in answering these questions is the difference between a profession or a job in the traditional world of work opposed to the modern business of network marketing. You can become and be extremely successful in both areas, but the psychological and thus also the mental foundations of both worlds are completely different and therefore, the fun factor accordingly has to be evaluated in a different way. If you earn your living and money as an employee, as most of our fellow human beings do, you are not only exchanging your time for money. You also trade freedom for authority and place yourself in a hierarchy to which you completely need to surrender. You can't choose your colleagues or your tasks yourself. You cannot decide who you will work with on a project. Nor what and on what you work. You can't even influence the time it takes. You will be told by when something must be finished. So as someone who is employed, you are always in a certain position of dependency and act as a tiny part in a chain of command. So, it's a matter of luck if you enjoy the tasks you're given. The same applies to your workplace and to the people in your team. Since you can't "pick and choose" them, you have no influence on who works with you. Here too, it takes a fair amount of luck if there is a perfect fit between you and your colleagues. But if you now look at the factor of fun at work and evaluate it in terms of its importance, you will notice what fun can achieve in professional life and in particular its role in your personal life.

First and foremost, fun is one of the most important motivators. If something is enjoyable, it means we like doing it, and when we like doing it, we want to do more of it. This is normal, a completely human emotional state. Fun is a driving force that people willingly expose themselves to. It is a positive pressure that spurs on and releases equally positive forces. Those who are actively having fun can therefore produce better results and considerably better achievement, which is reflected in their overall performance. Work that is done with joy and fun also is also easy to do. It doesn't stress you as much as if you really struggle through a pile of work. You would also perceive something like that to be a burden, and surely a pink feeling would not arise there. Work that doesn't suit you, that you don't like to do or that even overburdens you puts pressure on your mind, and ultimately puts you in a bad mood. Yes, it can even depress you and make you ill. In a worst-case scenario when the mental stress becomes too much, the brain and the body cannot really recover from the stress factors at all. Instead, you find yourself in a "hamster wheel" of permanent tension. This cannot go well in the long run and this constant overload can then lead to burnout, an illness that is increasingly mutating into a widespread epidemic. Having fun at work is easier said than done though, right? Nobody forces you to do anything in the network! You are free! You are your own determiner! It follows logically then, that you do not do anything that you do not like or that you do not enjoy. It is your life and your business - so live both with fun! Be pink in your head and in your heart. You will achieve this if you live up to your strengths and are motivated to do tasks that bring you joy. And that has consequences - positive ones for you and for your results, because only those who go to work full motivation and ready to have fun can achieve great things. Impressive results are always the result of enthusiasm, of joy in doing what you do.

Fun is thus an extremely important building block in the Pink:Code - after all, it influences one's own state of mind, the degree of positive thoughts, the intense experience of one's own actions and the resulting performance. Fun is the catalyst of creativity, the joy of creating, of work intensity, of speed. Speed through fun? Absolutely - because if what you have to do is easy and comfortable, it doesn't really bother you, and it doesn't weigh you down. And because of that, you automatically become faster - you start earlier, do it more efficiently, and therefore finish faster! In addition, fun supports your own diligence and inner resilience. It supports you even when things get difficult and leads you to top results. Because it lets you get into a flow that carries you along. Suddenly your work becomes almost like your hobby. Because the fun gives your work a lightness that many people only know from leisure activities.

And don't forget: Fun is contagious, just like pink is contagious! This means that if you are active with joy, if you approach challenges with a certain ease, you simply exude a "Pink-tastic vibe." Almost involuntarily, you will have a smile on your lips in all that you do with fun and joy. You put on a friendly face. And that's exactly what you will transmit to others, to all the partners in your team. Why? Because scientists now know that the mere facial expression of a smiling or even laughing person causes the brains of others to prepare their own facial muscles to smile or laugh along. This is an automatic process. You have to be in a really bad mood if you can resist this at all. That's why laughter is contagious. Even if you don't know the reason for the other person's smile. In this respect, pink is not only something personal, but fun at work becomes "pink for the people!"

2. THINK BIG – WITHOUT THINKING AT ALL

Think big is a common saying in the United States. Across the pond, people learn to think big from an early age. In Europe on the other hand, we have our own, often different understanding of this concept. Here, people tend to outwardly focus on latent modesty. To top it all off, the whole thing is then dubbed with the Anglicism "understatement." Somewhere along the lines of: "Be modest and show humility." And I urge you to discard this way of thinking right now. Say goodbye to it! Good riddance! My advice to you: Think big! Bigger than big! Let your visions run free. Break the boundaries of your thinking because you can't breathe freely in confined spaces. If you constantly imprison yourself and your dreams, hiding them under the uptight cloak of false modesty, how will you ever fulfill your desires? How are you going to set a great goal for yourself and achieve it if you're holding yourself back with this limited, narrow-minded thinking? Trying to achieve full speed with the handbrake on is like trying to fly with clipped wings. Why bother?

Thinking big requires putting an end to false, limiting social phrases and beliefs. Have you ever been asked the following question? "What do you want people to say or think about this?" It's a terrible phrase. Why? Because it makes it clear how constrained you can be. By conforming to the supposed tastes and opinions of others. You want to please others - but not yourself. Isn't that perfidious madness? It implies the following: It doesn't matter at all how I feel, the main thing is that others think and talk favorably about me. There is no more self-sacrifice than that. That's not pink, it's the epitome of being a "gray mouse."

Thinking big works the other way around. With presence, with a clear yes to one's own self and with the courage to step over one's own boundaries. Yes, even not to recognize these limits in the first place. Because who is supposed to show you limits? Only you can do that! A phrase that is often used in this context is: "I can't afford that!" Wrong! Turn the phrase around as a meaningful question and you'll be thinking pink: "What do I have to do to afford it?" It's not about the now, the in the moment, the immediately. Only about the "how!" But never about the "…I can't…!" One thing I have clearly recognized in my network life: Only those who think big can also achieve big. Because if you expect more, you get more in the end.

Thinking big has absolutely nothing to do with being crazy or even utopian. It is merely a measure of imagination. How are you going to achieve a big goal in your life if you can't even imagine it in your wildest dreams? It won't work, because just imagining it will make it impossible for you. Remember, what you don't dream, you can't wish for. Or as I like to say: Why do you dream of an apartment when you could have a beautiful house? The great visionary Walt Disney summed it up with his famous phrase: "If you can dream it, you can do it!"

Those who are in the Pink:Code infect others with pink instead of being plunged into darkness by the doom and gloom of others. Don't let yourself be talked down to, don't let yourself be swayed and manipulated by smooth talk. And if someone tries, raise your hand with a friendly smile and tell the other person, "I'm sorry you feel that way. But I invite you to come into my beautiful, positive world for once and think a little bigger too!" Bet you'll get open mouths and big surprises? Because no one expects such a reaction - this is also a way to think big by acting big!

Go just one step beyond your previous limits and you will see how big the world is - the mental and the real one. And that's what inspires you. It will give you incredible motivation. Because thinking big liberates. Suddenly you'll recognize completely new areas of possibility once you've looked beyond your personal limitations. It's like looking through a telescope that takes you into completely new worlds. Suddenly you realize for yourself what is possible, what could be. And from this realization, ideally many new goals can be defined. And ones that you haven't even recognized yet, precisely because you've never looked so far beyond your previous limits.

You can get into the habit of this way of thinking quite easily. The best way is to ask yourself every time what else might be possible or what might be the hidden potential behind your current goal. Is it still possible to go further? Is this already enough? You can only answer all these questions if you try. That is, when you start thinking big. For example, if you set the goal of a larger sum of money as your income and you are satisfied with this sum then you will never find out if more is actually possible because you're not tapping into your potential.

Thinking big also means pushing your own limits - and even going beyond the horizon of possibilities. The good thing about it is that the effort is and remains the same - only the results will get better and bigger. Because it's just as easy to think small or mediocre as it is to rely on the Pink:Code, to leave the limits behind and switch to "think big." For those who internalize this and question their visions repeatedly, big thinking becomes a mantra.

There is an ancient quote that sums it up when it comes to great thinking and the corresponding automatism: "Watch your thoughts, for they become words. Watch your words, for they become actions. Watch your actions, for they become habits..." Welcome to the Pink:Code is all I can say. Think big without thinking about it, that's the point. You just have to make yourself aware of thinking big and reflection also helps you to do that - but that's the next characteristic that belongs to the Pink key.

3. REFLECTION & INTUITION

Honestly, do you truly know yourself? Do you know who you are? Do you have an idea of how you affect others and how you come across to others? Do you know how you think, what makes you tick and what your attitude is? Well, are you wavering right now when you think about it? Are you suddenly not so sure anymore? That's not necessarily a bad thing, because that's what happens to most people who think about these questions a bit more intensively for the first time. Of course, at first glance everyone is inclined to claim with conviction that they know themselves.

Taking the time to reflect on yourself, your way of thinking, feeling, and behaving can be an incredibly enlightening process. It is not about discovering supposed mistakes. Rather, reflection helps to change something where it makes sense and to focus even more on one's own strengths. If you ask yourself once what you are doing right, you will be surprised what is possible afterwards. Every response is praise in its own right and still demonstrates how much potential for growth there is. There is still more to do, despite the good or even very good results so far. You are virtually already pink, but you can intensify the color and make it glow and shine even more.

While I talked about the importance of thinking big in the previous paragraph, reflection also helps you to achieve greater dimensions in your thinking itself. Because if you get to know yourself even better, you will also be able to see and define your own goals more clearly and you will also discover that you probably do things differently than others. If that's the case, then I can only congratulate you. Great! Because just because many others do something the way they do it, doesn't mean it's the best way. And it especially doesn't have to be your way. But that's exactly what you need to question critically. The phrase "We've always done it this way" is nothing more than personal capitulation to the better alternative. It is a mindset of mental stagnation, combined with fear or even cowardice of the new or the different.

Why is this important? For one, it can be a confirmation that what you have done and how you have practiced it is correct. Great, you're already on the right track. However, it may also lead to a different outcome. This demonstrates that you can reach your goal more quickly or make the journey less challenging for yourself, which results in even more fun and ease. Just as you have learned from the previous paragraphs, it's all the same thing. You see, constantly questioning yourself has many advantages. And if you leave the mainstream behind, sometimes all it takes is changing small things in your doing and thinking. It is exactly like going from a well-trodden path used by many to a still unused, perfectly constructed, brand new asphalted highway. More comfort, more freedom, and new perspectives on the horizon would be the result.

I'm deliberately not using the metaphor of "swimming against the current" because that sounds more like a mere act of defiance. "I don't want to be like everyone else, so I'm turning around and deliberately working against everyone else!" That's not the purpose of being and experiencing off the mainstream. Because the benefits would only be being different. Standing out, standing out from the crowd - there's nothing wrong with that, but you have to decide whether you want that and what it's useful for. If you consciously "swim against the current", you also accept a greater effort, namely to fight against the force of the current that flows against you. If this is neither necessary nor accompanied by great benefits, then you might as well save yourself some energy and use it for other things that cater to your needs.

On the other hand, it can be much more important to change your perspective, to question things, processes, automatisms, and ways of acting and to think the other way around. This is a fundamental aspect of reflection and involves a mental clearing-out process. It requires examining one's actions or approaches and eliminating those that are outdated or ineffective. You question the benefits achieved, the effort put in and the final effectiveness. All of this brings you closer to an ideal state, which is to become the best version of yourself. This is the Pink:Code in its almost complete form.

What does that mean? Put simply: It is about doing the right thing without having to think about it explicitly. Your gut feeling tells you what to do – and then what you do is right. You make decisions without having to reflect beforehand. Rather, you act from your experiences, from what you can do, what you know and who you are. Sounds mystical, doesn't it? But it isn't. There are so many decisions you make for yourself day after day without thinking long and hard about it. You simply act because your instincts tell you it's the right thing to do. And intuition is one of the most reliable feelings we have. It's like an inner compass that captures individual aspects faster than any reflection, which are relevant for the final evaluation and decision. It brings together many perspectives that have already played a role in your life and were somehow important. They are the already acquired experiences that are collected and evaluated - and that are decided upon from the gut.

Whether it concerns your way of thinking, the joy of doing, or your positive outlook - the more intensely you engage with these aspects, as well as with yourself, the more experience you anchor within your inner self. This mindset will become second nature to you. As a result, you will also develop increasing intuition - you will assess and decide almost automatically correctly. But of course, you are also pink!

4. LEARN TO UNLEARN & BE BRAVE

Only those who are open to new things, who remain open-minded and willing to gain new experiences, will also be able to develop further. This is the surest way to avoid stagnation or even regression in any respect. It also requires a certain amount of courage to discard previous habits and ways of doing things and to renounce old theories by following a growth mindset. Not because they are necessarily wrong, but because new, more modern approaches turn out to be the more effective and efficient methods.

This valuable willingness to generally allow something new is therefore just as much a question of courage. Even more so when it comes to trying out new things. You need to leave your comfort zone, perhaps even force yourself to do so to some extent. Why? Because the past and present gave you safety and comfort. It has become comfortable because it has worked well so far. But couldn't it be even better, because the supposedly new thing offers many more advantages? Wouldn't that make the results even better? Wouldn't you and your team benefit even more from it? Finally, if only one of these questions is answered with yes, then a new process is set in motion: rethinking and relearning! Experts like to talk about reskilling in this context!

It is very courageous to admit at a certain point in time that one should do things differently than before, especially when it seems that the new approach is better and promises better results. But what is courageous about this realization? Undoubtedly, the better approach should always replace the old one. Because we all know: Perfect is the enemy of good! Easier said than done. Because it is precisely at this moment that the previous, tried and tested, proven and perhaps even cherished habits stand in the way of the new action. But if you follow the Pink:Code, you know what to do: Rethink! Think anew! And discard previous habits, practices and automatisms and replace them with new ones. A process that is understood in the Pink:Code as: Learn to unlearn!

What was once good, always remains good! This is precisely the kind of thinking that acts as a roadblock to progress and development. Network marketing and the Pink:Code live from the desire to learn, to experience new things and to be constantly in the process of progress. But in the end, we are all "creatures of habit" and like to stay stuck in old structures. Do you feel the same way? Letting go of familiar processes and routines and learning new methods and behaviors that are tailored to the situation and task at hand can be extremely difficult. Interestingly, many people find it easier to learn new things than to unlearn old habits. Why is that? Mainly because synaptic connections, i.e. frequently used connections in the brain, are difficult to break. These brain connections are in direct competition with the new.

And yet, especially in the network marketing industry, it is essential to embrace the new, the progressive, and to go with it. Without compromise. "New" does not mean "previously undiscovered and freshly developed." "New" means above all "different in relation to previous habits." Because what may be practical outside the network may not be practical within the network. Because this industry is modern, but just as fast-moving. It continues to develop from day to day, because new people are always bringing in new and different ideas and creative approaches to unheard solutions.

When I said at the beginning that in this wonderful business you can always learn something new, that also means being curious - and staying curious! Curiosity is a positive form of interest and shows open-mindedness. It describes the desire to discover something, to want to know more than before and thus to bring oneself to a new, higher level. If these new experiences and observations are then possibly diametrically opposed to all the previous routines and habits, then it is a matter of relearning! Unlearn the old to learn the new!

This is a real challenge, as previous processes and ways of thinking tend to collide with the new automatisms, which first have to be recreated in the mind and then become more and more established as a ritual. Maybe you even know this challenge from sports? For me, it is still one of the most striking examples and comes from the field of athletics - the high jump. For years, athletes in this discipline almost universally jumped over the bar using the straddle technique. With the upper body in front, the bar was jumped over by means of an oblique roll on the stomach. The jumper rolled forward on landing. But then came the 1968 Olympics, and American athlete Dick Fosbury made his appearance. When he jumped, athletes and experts could not believe their eyes. The special thing about this jumping technique was that he crossed the bar backwards. So Fosbury didn't start straight but ran a curve and turned around just before the bar, so that his back crossed the bar first. Since that moment, all high jumpers have jumped with this technique and that meant they had to completely relearn it at the beginning.

Or think of the ski jumpers. Until the 1990s, they had to keep their skis tight and parallel to each other during the flight. And today? The opposite is the case. Today, everyone forms a V when flying with their skis. And again, back then it was a matter of forgetting the old, accepting the new and relearning. They all had to learn to unlearn to learn the new!

Do you remember what you read a few paragraphs earlier when I wrote about thinking big - without thinking about it explicitly? That's an aspect that matters here too. Because if you embrace the new without reservation, if you do, instead of merely thinking about it, if you unlearn the old in order to implement the new without thinking, then your Pink levels will become more and more intense. Why? Because you can now fully utilize the key "Pink." You know what it means to be pink. Because you're having fun, thinking big beyond your limits, always reflecting, and open to progress because you've mastered the art of learning by unlearning. These four characteristics make up the Pink Key - the first of eight steps to deciphering the Pink:Code! You are on the right track…

GENERAL RULE: LESS THINKING, MORE DOING!

SMILE, AND THE WILL CHANGE.

MORE FREEDOM AND STANDING UP FOR YOURSELF

Later my involvement and assistance in my parent's business shifted more to the restaurant, which my parents rebuilt on a plot of land next to the campsite and really led to success. Our restaurant was popular and known all over Lake Constance, and there was no question that my brother and I would be involved accordingly. Help within the family should be an inner purpose. After all, this also promotes integrity and in turn shapes one's own responsibility towards others. Yes, I can say that I grew up with work, which did me no harm.

I gradually realized how important and valuable it is to take a moment to breathe. I use the word "allow" intentionally, to emphasize that one truly has the time completely to oneself-- which is not a given for everyone nowadays. That means having the freedom to make decisions during this time without the pressure of other obligations, without worrying about what others expect of me or who is waiting for me. It's leisure time, time without any pressure, without hearing a clock ticking in the background. That's a precious commodity that you must create and preserve. This is exactly what I have found in network marketing. I was finally able to experience this said freedom here.

As a child, I didn't perceive my parents' business as work, but as I grew older, it increasingly collided with my own interests. I couldn't attend events, hangouts, parties from the beginning because I was always required to help out in the restaurant. So, I always arrived much later to events than everyone else. I didn't miss such parties completely, but when you're always the last to arrive, it's hard to get involved in the conversations, the hustle and bustle, and the happy, boisterous celebratory mood. The older I got, the more clearly, I realized that this business, which my parents ran with dedication, was certainly not meant to be my future, and since I was a good student with equally good grades, I also knew that the world was my oyster. I just had to find the right door and unlock it.

Yes, I wanted to take the next step - also because I felt it was time. I had to move on, move forward and open the next door in my life! And this door for me was called: Obtaining a university degree! Especially since there had always been a latent desire in me to rise to higher social spheres. I wanted to work my way up. This desire was also because we were at home in an environment that, on the one hand, is one of the most beautiful corners of Lake Constance but on the other hand, only people who could afford to live in the most beautiful spot in the area lived around the campground. Hence, families with the corresponding income whose children were in a class with me and who, for example, bought fresh rolls from me at the kiosk on Sundays.

But hold on! Whoever now assumes that I experience some form of social envy is wrong. Nothing could be further away from the truth. There was also no reason for it because I was fully accepted in this social circle. Nevertheless, I noticed that there were differences. Be it clothes, their hobbies or the opportunities that were offered to them. For this reason alone, I had set myself the goal early on to get ahead in life and swore to myself: today you buy rolls from me, but one day I will turn the tables. I'm going to make it. And my grandmother encouraged me in my endeavors by telling me again and again, "You just have to be diligent, and then you can do anything, because no one can resist diligence!" A great motto! It is not a matter of qualities, talent or certain physical stamina, but of diligence. That is something that everyone can leverage because you can't say, "Too bad, I'd love to be diligent, but I just can't!" Everyone can be diligent and thus achieve something!

The ultimate achievement however, comes from a certain combination: Diligence in conjunction with a driving force that triggers incredible energy and undreamed-of powers. This will, which is determined by a clearly defined, individual purpose, lets you do what is necessary with full focus - even if it becomes unpleasant at times. You climb over hurdles that seemed previously insurmountable. This power pushes you forward. I realized this at the time I told my parents that I wanted to study after I had done very well in my high school exams. Enthusiasm looks different when I think about my father's first reaction. He had already secretly envisaged me in the role of the person who would continue the family's gastronomic business. And now this. His daughter wanted to become an academic, instead of a business-owner!

After sophomore year at the high school in Radolfzell, I transferred to a business high school in Constance. This was also because my father regarded me as someone who should be professionally competent to take over his business one day. Bookkeeping and account management, payroll and invoicing, as well as foreign languages (something I was already good at), were added on top of the usual curriculum. The requirements there were pretty much in line with my skills. It was a good fit! In addition, many of my peers from the old high school also wanted to leave the school and go to the business high school. Great, then we would have all been reunited I thought. What I did not consider at the time was that there were two business high schools in the area- one in Singen and one in Constance. So, when my first day at the new school started, I immediately noticed that none of my old classmates were in my new school. My mind was filled with question marks. "Where was everyone?" I asked myself. "They all wanted to go to the business high school, too! Right?" And my former classmates also kept their word, but still there was no sign of them at my new school. And then I slowly understood. They had all enrolled in Singen. So, from then on, I was the only one to attend school in Constance. We had agreed on something, but apparently not clearly or distinctly enough.

But the school was also a hit for me. I was able to use all my strengths here and found ways into the arts, where I was able to live out my creative streak to the fullest. Wonderful! Or almost too wonderful. Because suddenly the desire matured in me to continue my studies in the liberal arts. And this was then the plan I openly shared with my parents. Scandalous – not only did I thwart my father's plans of taking over the business, now I also wanted to major in art – and not even management studies. Or as he called it in his parlance: "fruitless art", because he immediately saw me as an impoverished painter in front of a wildly painted canvas - many blots on my painter's smock, but not a cent in my wallet. We therefore made a compromise - also for the sake of general family peace -: A major in business administration. Not my desired subject, but at least a step in the right direction towards studying.

With big dreams and an extremely small budget, I went to beautiful Regensburg, almost 400 kilometers away. Money? No, not a dime in my pocket. My parents had only given me the opportunity to earn some extra money at their house on weekends. Other than that, I received nothing that I did not work for. My father made it unmistakably clear to me that there were no funds left to finance my studies. Hence, I did what I had always done anyway: Work! In Regensburg on Tuesday's I worked in gastronomy as a counter worker and on weekends, I was busy waitressing at my parents' restaurant. In short: I was in action around the clock.

Yes, my budget was always tight, but I always managed to make ends meet. And my grandmother always passed over a little bit of cash here and there, which was then usually reinvested for the next full tank of gas for my car. But anyone who knows what it's like when money is permanently tight appreciates the real importance and the associated freedom of money even more. Money is not important? Whoever says something like that doesn't know what it's like not having any. A person with this mindset doesn't know what kind of liberation you feel when you do have money in the bank, even if it is only sparse, and you can only pay for things that need to be paid for. Money is and remains pure freedom because it makes life worth living.

This has nothing to do with abundance or luxury. Not at all. But it makes it possible to get to know the good, the beautiful sides of life. Therefore, we in Europe should finally get used to a much more laid-back way of dealing with money. We should all accept it as something that is good, that can create positive value, and that frees us, makes us more independent, and thus also makes us a little happier. More diligence and striving for more financial freedom and satisfaction would certainly be better than constantly preached social envy. Because one thing is clear: Only a person who feels fully content on the inside, can also be a good person!

For six semesters, my life ran at a stressful, breathless pace. One day in Regensburg, the other day in Lake Constance. One minute on campus, the next behind the counter. One minute I was in the lecture hall, and a few hours later I was back serving food at my parents' business, running around with a friendly smile on my face. And to top it all off, I had even managed to pass my pre-degree in business administration. Everything went according to plan, and in the end, I graduated with a degree in business administration. But sometimes things turn out differently than you expect and plan. Life always has a surprise in store when you least expect it and this was exactly what happened to me. The surprise that brought about a turn of events that I would hardly have thought possible before.

It all happened in a small artist supply store in Munich. Paints, brushes, canvases - no, I hadn't quite lost my old love and passion for painting and art. Sure, I had perhaps swallowed my pride and accepted the fact that I had traded my art studies for a business degree, but my inner inclination towards beauty remained. Numbers, data, and facts can be as meaningful as they are, but they can in no way compete with the beauty of the arts, nor do they have to. And because I always liked to go into this extraordinary atmosphere, to get a whiff of this special artist's air and to immerse myself in the painter and art ambience, I visited this wonderful store in the Bavarian capital on my way back from Regensburg. But as soon as I entered the store, I could not believe my eyes ...

I met an old school friend with whom I had graduated high school and had not seen or spoken to since. What a warm reunion and of course one with the usual questions. Where do you live now? What is going on in your love life? What are you doing now? I told her about my rather boring field of study and all the stress surrounding it, before my friend told me about her university's faculty with enthusiasm. She was enrolled at the University of Applied Sciences in Constance and was studying communication design there! "It's fun! It's great! It's creative! It has a future!" She never stopped raving about how happy she was. And as the real "cherry on top" she invited me to her campus: "We have an 'open campus day' next weekend. Just come and have a look, and you'll even have the chance to talk to one of the professors!" she added. I was "on fire."

Business administration? Forget it! Regensburg? Forgotten! Intermediate diploma? Forgotten! My fellow alumnus had really managed to inspire me with a few words and stories filled with enthusiasm. She ignited a fire in me, the embers of which had probably never been completely extinguished. This was probably one of the reasons why the surprising encounter in the artist's store turned into an intensive exchange lasting more than three hours in a nearby café. I wanted to know everything, I was curious, and thirsty for knowledge. When we said goodbye, one thing was clear to me: Something had changed in me. This meeting had opened my eyes. And it had opened my eyes to a very specific truth: Be yourself! It's your turn and from now on, follow your heart! I would have loved to shout this realization out from the rooftops. The feeling was so strong, this inner liberation that overcame me. It was a release, one that finally made me see clearly. From now on, it was clear to me: I will not make any lazy compromises - not for others, nor against myself!

Follow your heart – this is how you remain true to yourself

1. Sketch out your personal path to follow your heart in detail. Where do you stand? Where are you starting from? Where do you really want to go? And which stops are on your way?

2. What hurdles and obstacles can lie in your way? What challenges can you overcome yourself with your existing skills and resources? Are there any that you need help with?

3. Be clear about the reason why you want to follow your heart. Even the simplest motive, the smallest reason can be enough!

4. Come to realize that you alone, are the most important person in your life. Therefore, you must also be happy with yourself.

5. Self-love is good for self-confidence and has nothing to do with selfishness or egocentricity. Be your biggest fan!

6. Only if you love yourself can you love others. But you can only love yourself if you are also true to yourself. Make this clear to yourself again and again and ask yourself whether you really adhere to this advice.

7. Remember: If you make yourself a priority, you are authentic and honest.

8. Always trust in what you can do - build on your strengths. Who cares about your supposed weaknesses? Certainly not you!

9. Examine your own beliefs. Do they help or hinder you?

10. Be aware: Self-confidence does not come from always being right, but from not being afraid to be wrong.

2nd Key: **POSITIVE**

To have a fundamentally positive attitude is one thing above all not a miracle and certainly not mental mumbo-jumbo. Having a consistently positive perspective is rather a concept and a personal agreement with yourself. It's about seeing the good in life first and saying yes to life. That is what it is all about, and to be clear: If you have a positive attitude, you don't automatically see everything only through the famous rose-colored glasses. Although this would actually fit wonderfully to the Pink:Code. Positive thinking, actually includes an absolute sense of reality. In fact, it is extremely important to always make reasonable decisions based on prior reflection. This does not mean that one is trying to find something positive in even the worst tragedy, or about talking oneself out of an extremely unfortunate personal situation. In this case, you would refer to this as being blind to the truth, naive or dreaming unrealistically. With senseless utopia, one wins nothing except the loss of their own grounding. Positive thinking is rather a form of savvy coping as well as the skill to better process negative events and situations. How do I react and what does such a negative event do to me?

Unfortunately, life does not only consist of days full of sunshine. We all know that. It's just a question of how to deal with the "rainy days." Do you allow yourself to be dragged down to the depths of despair? So deep that you could really bury yourself in it? Can you even read the bad mood on your face, because the corners of your mouth are pointing menacingly downward, and your vision is clouded? Do you look like a "heap of misery?" Or do you straighten up with a go-getter attitude to fight against the mental gloom and defy the bad mood? Do you internalize the old saying: "There will be sunshine after the rain?" In short: Are you an optimist or do you belong to the pessimist camp? Nobody is born as one or the other. No one sees the light of day and can be happy to be an "optimism baby." Science has now discovered that a maximum of 25 percent of a positive or negative attitude to life is innate. This means, in turn, that around 75 per cent are still unattributed and thus freely definable! In fact, the first four years of our life in particular, determine whether we will be a a resilient individual or someone who falls and remains down in the future.

But the good news is: Despite all the "precoding" in childhood, even the biggest pessimist is not a hopeless case, because positive thinking and a positive attitude towards life, can be learned. No one is trapped in a negative mindset forever. You can get out of it - if you want to. However, and this is unfortunately part of the truth as well, many pessimists don't want to. Why? Because a negative attitude and view is also a bit comfortable, because you passively move into a negative comfort zone: into the role of the victim! Pessimists prefer to retreat into a sulking corner and simply let negative occurrences happen to them - without stepping up for themselves. The counterintuitively pleasant thing about being a "sourpuss" is that you are almost always right. If something doesn't work as expected, then every pessimist will immediately react with the sentence: "I told you so!" Or: "See, I knew it all along…!" But even if the tide is turning or a situation is positive, pessimists prefer to claim that they are somehow still right, but immediately add their negative touch to it. Preferably with profane sentences such as "That was purely a matter of luck this time" Those who are fundamentally negative and thus pessimistic, just make things a bit easier for themselves. It has been scientifically proven today: Negative thoughts and events outweigh positive ones in our brain and hence stick more easily and, unfortunately, often longer. At the same time, it is the reason why bad news sells considerably better than good news.

But even if it's not always easy, it's worth facing negative events openly, consciously, and curiously instead of with fear and gloomy thoughts. This includes, for example, not allowing oneself to be flooded with negative news, in times and situations of crisis. It is better to explicitly inform oneself about certain events and to take breaks from the wave of information in between. It is enough to learn about a disaster once and not several times a day. This helps to replenish your energy reserves. Even better, simply turn off the TV and the news. Adopt this motto: Better no news than bad news. The same goes for daily newspapers. It's not that important or valuable to hear about the next war, the next tragedy, or the next catastrophe multiple times a day. This does not mean you are ignoring reality, you're just someone who doesn't let anything negative get to you. Sometimes it's simply a matter of banning negativity from your own life and daily routine. That can alone be positive enough. This also applies to conscious contact with people who are rather optimistic. Why bother with people who are always complaining? What value does it bring you? None! You are not the garbage dump of other people who fill you up with their problems and negative thoughts. In the end, you give them your energy. Probably even so much of it that they feel considerably better in the end - but not you. You then need to see how you can free yourself from the "mental garbage" and crawl out from under the "pile of pessimism" in order to be able to turn to positive thoughts again. You make it possible for others to live at the expense of your good mood. Why? Think about yourself and your own smile. Everything else is an unnecessary hassle. And therefore: You don't need to do it. It is not helpful!

Someone who thinks positively have fine-tuned their perspective. That's someone who can focus and look for the good and they also usually find it, because such a person has the required willpower to find positive things. They look for the pink in life and don't look for the gray or black. These people hold an important piece of the second key to the "pink happiness" in their hands. "Thoughts are free" as quoted in an old German song. That's right and that's why you alone decide what color they are. That's why it's best to choose pink!

THE FOUR MOST IMPORTANT FEATURES, THAT DEFINE THE KEY: **POSITIVITY**

1. THE ART OF INDULGING

Who has not dreamed of becoming rich through the efforts of others? You can be honest about this because that's perfectly okay. Without actively intervening, your bank balance and your own career grow. Great, isn't it? What a nice thought and the best part about this thought is that it's not even completely out of the blue, because such things do exist. It's not a miracle, it's not just wishful thinking, and it's not just a fantasy because basically, the network marketing system fulfills exactly this unique wish. You only have one thing to do: Offer others the chance to participate in the business and then help them to become successful. Preferably even more successful than you are. That is the real pivotal point. Make others rich and you become rich yourself. Make others successful and you become successful yourself. Make others happy and you become happy. In a way, network marketing is nothing else than the realization of the old biblical wisdom: "Give and it will be given to you!"

The only prerequisite in this context is the art of taking a step back and letting others bask in the limelight. In short: One must be able to give! With this compassionate mindset, you are automatically the perfect opposite of envy, resentment, and self-importance, because in the network, the wise rule applies: "Reduce your stature to increase your influence!" That's supposed to be a contradiction, right? No, not at all. Rather, it is a sign of greatness, self-confidence, and personal competence. Because only those who know what they can do, who count on themselves and build on themselves, will also have the strength to help others reach their goals. On the other hand, those who stumble and are not at peace with themselves do not have the energy to support others and help them along one stage or another.

Imagine a long-distance runner who is slowly but surely running out of breath. Suddenly he sees someone else on the track in front of him who, out of exhaustion can no longer continue. Someone who can hardly stand on his own two feet. How is someone without any more energy of his own supposed to help this other person to the finishing line? How is he supposed to support him and encourage him to keep running? This just simply won't work. His inner voice is asking him to think of himself. Someone like that only thinks about crossing the finish line himself, about using his remaining strength well and only for himself, to perhaps secure a place for themselves on the winner's podium. There is no more room for others in one's thoughts. The thoughts revolve egoistically around how to somehow reach the goal. Help others? Never ever! And yes, maybe such a person will just make it over the finish line - and then? He will remain alone with his result despite the struggle against himself. Tomorrow, this small victory will be forgotten and so will he. But how would the result have been, if this person with self-confidence and personal greatness had instead grabbed the other person or put their arm around them and both of them would have made it to the finish line together? What kind of lasting victory would that have been? Something that people would still have been talking about weeks later. If this person had placed less importance on himself, there would probably have been two winners instead of just one who somehow made it. One has exchanged a minimal victory for a great triumph at that moment.

Quite different is a personality of integrity that can rely on its own skills. They have already achieved their own successes, have tasted the sweet nectar of victory, and triumphed many times and know how good it feels and tastes. Such a person possesses self-confidence and also self-assurance. This personality acts out of its own strength. It rejoices when others rejoice because that is true greatness. Something that is of fundamental importance in network marketing. Because only those who help others, who form a real team, who live and exemplify teamwork, who lead others to victory and make them successful, will in the end profit from it to the highest degree. This is the core of the system. Perhaps even the actual secret of success.

Only those who can grant something to others, who can be happy for others, can also claim a piece of happiness for themselves. If, on the other hand, you always walk around with the formula in your head "Me first and then the others," you will get in your own way. Why? Because one's ego puts up a wall around one's own person. This is an important aspect because when it comes to network marketing, to give something to others does not necessarily mean envy. Rather, envy arises when people constantly compare themselves with everyone and everything else. In the network, "being able to indulge" means sharing, giving, and letting others go first or reaching out to them and taking their hand. Putting your own self in the background here and there, to make room to offer others the stage. It is not an art, but a skill with a pinch of decency and morality that can - and should - be learned. But to do that, you obviously must come to terms with yourself first. Accepting that other people can also do certain things or perform accordingly – it does not have to work against you but has the potential to actually work in your favor.

It almost goes without saying that doing so requires a certain inner strength. Without self-confidence, this will be difficult to achieve. This is the only way to show greatness in small things. But how do you do that? By first showing greatness and magnanimity to yourself. Because sometimes we tend to be way too hard on ourselves. Be fair to yourself for a change, is all I can say because if you know you've done your best, then you have nothing to blame yourself for. And what is your best? The maximum that you are capable of. But that doesn't mean you have to always surpass yourself. This aspiration can motivate you and increase your self-confidence, but if you overdo it, you'll end up in a dangerous downward spiral, frustratedly chasing after your goals and failing every time.

An exaggerated sense of ego, any forms of egomania and self-importance are an unpleasant accumulation of erroneous vanity. True human greatness on the other hand, enhances our prestige and respect. It makes us likeable and attractive. It also increases confidence in us and, finally, even elevates us to be a role model. However, true greatness is not a quality that we acquire or learn once and then possess forever. Greatness must be lived. Daily! Quite a few people succumb to the misconception that they become greater by making others smaller. Such a person reveals at best a low self-esteem and a veritable sense of neurosis. The correct formula reads exactly the other way around: True greatness makes others great! Self-worth and greatness however, are not relative qualities, but they are absolute. You don't gain more of them by depriving others of their greatness or by defending your own value in order to look better. These are all signs of weakness. Those who are truly great allow others to grow or rejoice in their greatness. True greatness is always directed at others. It is about recognizing the greatness of others and promoting their achievements. And never forget in network marketing, that's exactly what pays off - in two respects. Psychologists say that true greatness does not demand or expect anything in return. In the network industry it is a positive, pleasant side effect. As the performance of your team grows, so does your success and that of your upline. In this respect, what counts is: "As long as you try to make yourself bigger by making others smaller, you'll have doubts about your greatness." You could also say that as long as you are trying to cover up the pink in others, you're still quite gray yourself!

2. EXPECT NOTHING, GIVE EVERYTHING!

Those who have expectations, hope for rewards as a result of their actions. If this reward is not promised or if there is no reason to hope for it, the intensity of commitment will probably also decrease noticeably. Basically, this means nothing other than that one is only willing to do something if one receives an adequate reward in return. That is exactly the description of expectations. What a pressure one thus builds up for oneself and shoulders in the process. With each expectation, the resulting outcome becomes irrefutable. I put something in so that something else comes out. But what happens when that very result is not achieved? And that can happen more often than you think. After all, life is not a fixed-interest savings plan where you can predict the result at the end with compound interest after a fixed term. This insight is also justified in network marketing - and even more so in the Pink:Code. You don't know how a customer will react until you have approached them about your product. You also don't know whether they will recognize the opportunity you are offering them as such and choose to seize it in the moment. So why do you have expectations?

An attitude of expectations means that when the unexpected happens, disappointment usually follows, as well as dissatisfaction and doubts about one's own abilities. Expectations always have two sides. They can be fulfilled - or not! Certain expectations in life, in one's career and in one's success are important and meaningful. They provide orientation, ensure a certain reliability. No one is in a position to adjust and readjust every day. One would lose their inner compass and own orientation over time. But: Expectations that are too high cause inner stress. In addition, they are constricting because in the end there is little opportunity left to give chance even a little room.

Stress, pressure, compulsion - who needs that? Nobody. So just throw all your expectations overboard. Invest in yourself and your qualities, your power, your strengths, your commitment without any reservations and do it without expecting a return on your investment. This is called being unconditional, no strings attached, which in turn means a great deal more freedom for you. After all, expectations are basically nothing more than conditions that you place on yourself when in doubt. Flip the switch and say to yourself, "I'll just do it!" and then let yourself be surprised at how high "your return" will be. This way of thinking and acting has a huge advantage: If you don't expect anything, you can't be disappointed and least of all by yourself!

This is a real inner liberation from mental shackles. You will take the pressure off yourself and be able to start the day much more freely and that in turn generates an enormous and noticeable energy boost through increased motivation. To simply do without pressure, to go ahead and to give everything - that is real freedom. You become an inspiration for others because your freedom also lets others become much more relaxed and uninhibited. You take the pressure off their shoulders and allow them to move forwards together with you, without conditions, and all of this only because you give everything and expect nothing. It doesn't just sound good, it is good because with this mindset, you're putting a positive roof over yourself and your team. Honestly, how can anyone be positive if they're and moaning and groaning under the weight of the burden that they're carrying? It is the expectations that are placed on someone that can really crush them. They make every step more difficult and turn the actual joy of doing something into a burden.

Someone who is positive feels the breath of freedom. Such a person can breathe deeply and freely – because of their experienced positivity. Setting goals, defining individual hopes and dreams, and doing so clearly and distinctly is is important and correct. Now you are ready to give everything because your actions are no longer tied to any conditions and thus, expectations do not threaten you with any future negative consequences. On the contrary: You recognize "rosy prospects" by thinking positively because you give everything and expect nothing more. And now you have turned the second key of the Pink:Code a little further bringing the lock to the bigger picture closer to being opened!

3. START TODAY, RATHER THAN TOMORROW!

Do you know the story of the lazybones who, despite good intentions, never got around to becoming physically active? It's a story about the "insidious tomorrow" and how it keeps you from finally getting started. To start and get going, instead of postponing one's actions over and over again. Are you feeling stuck right now because you always like to feel that way? Well, read this story and you'll realize how everyone - including you - can come off the starting blocks.

A man couldn't and wouldn't really want to get excited about anything: He preferred to embrace his laziness. He was particularly fond of his armchair and the remote control for his television and streaming service. Oh, it was cozy and with a bit of cake, some chips and Coke every day, he was really enjoying himself. His wife, on the other hand, was a completely different kind of person. She was active, took care of the household with commitment, kept everything clean and tidy and earned good money as well. No wonder, she had a desire for success and was ambitious. Laziness? No, that was not her world.

What an unlikely couple. The lazy man, however was well-aware of how his wife had her life under control. She looked dazzling, had an athletic figure and not just by chance but because she took care of her body, with exercise, care, and hygiene. He, on the other hand, noticed how he was getting fatter and fatter, sluggish and even more tired. All was well until one day, his wife sat down with him on the couch and said, "I saw you got on the scale this morning and noticed how many kilos you've gained. You must do something, it's not healthy the way you live!" she admonished him. His response, "Okay, if you say so. From tomorrow, I'll start going for a little walk outside!"

But what happened the next day? Nothing! And not for the next few days either. He always had the same excuse ready when his wife asked him why he hadn't done anything again today. His response was always: "Tomorrow! Today I forgot!" When a week had passed, she approached her husband again - and he vowed to do better. This time he decided to trick himself and do something about forgetting. So, he took a bucket of red paint, a thick brush and climbed onto the bed with it. He then painted a reminder in red on the ceiling above his bed and which said in big letters: Don't forget - tomorrow you start! Nothing has been done and nothing has changed to this day. Why? Because every morning when he opened his eyes the ceiling read: "...Tomorrow you start...!"

Why always tomorrow instead of today? Why do we like to lie to ourselves so much? Isn't that strange? Even though we might even know the consequences of our own actions if we decide to start to change something tomorrow instead of today. Is it only the comfort, not to do something, although the resolution was to begin now? Everyone can do something against this fatal "procrastination. You just have to start.

Those who keep avoiding the decision to start something now, today, instead of tomorrow, are acting just like someone who is standing at the train station, actually wanting to leave on time in order to arrive punctually, but nevertheless just keeps letting one train after the next pass by - without getting on! Insane, isn't it? There are many reasons to act so carelessly and, in a way, irresponsibly. This inconsistent behavior even goes from a bad habit to a downright psychological work disorder. But if you recognize it yourself and know that you at least have the tendency to postpone until tomorrow, then you are already an honest step ahead. But what can you do to become a now-type and to leave the postponement behind you? Ideally, you should write down the things you want to do today and cross them off when they are done. And you hang up this list exactly where you can permanently keep an eye on it Why? Because then you feel guilty if you haven't done something from your list today and it's a kind of motivation, maybe even a bit of a reward, when you see all the things you've already crossed off. That's how you recognize what you've accomplished. It is like a small reward that motivates you to continue. If you don't want to write a list, you can also use photos or pictures that represent what needs to be done because psychologically, a picture has 60,000 times more impact on the subconscious than a single written word!

People who like to procrastinate usually don't have very good time management either. That's why the Pink:Code applies the clever technique: Take your time for something by setting yourself a start time and also a time by you want to be finished. The time span can be a bit more ambitious and therefore not too generous. This way, you'll also realize that the day still has enough time in store for you, so you can also relax. What a great reward. The greatest recognition for yourself however, is when you write down the resulting gains and successes to go along with your plans. This is not only motivating, but also gratifying because then you also know all the good things you get out of your activities.

Can you imagine what a feeling like that does to you? Exactly, you will be in a good mood because you have not only accomplished something, no, you have also defeated yourself. Especially your subconscious, which wanted to seduce you into comfort. But if that were it. It had much more sinister intentions in mind. It even wanted to take away all the good gains and successes by tempting you with comfort. Do you realize now how valuable it is to start now instead of later? And as a bonus on top of that, if you act this way, you will only gain advantages from it and absolutely zero disadvantages. Do you know what that does to you? Well, sure, you become even more positive bit by bit. You know that nothing and no one can stop you now. Without a doubt, your self-esteem and confidence - both personally and professionally - will skyrocket because you know what you can do and, above all, what you have already achieved - quite a lot. You owe it all to yourself - you and your abilities. Do you still think you want to wait and start tomorrow? Certainly not, because why wait to bask in success and celebrate triumphs later when you can do it right now! So, your Pink:Code slogan from now on is: Don't wait, start now!

4. THE ART OF CONSTANTLY THINKING POSITIVELY

Successful athletes know: Getting to the top is a challenge; staying at the top is the next and far greater challenge. At first glance, that doesn't sound very plausible. Doesn't it have to be much more arduous and require more energy to work your way from the very bottom to the very top?

The reality is different and if you take a closer look, it is understandable. Because anyone who wants to get to the top has a clear goal in mind. They know where the "finishing line" is and how to get there. Anyone who wants to reach the top knows exactly what requirements must be met and which parameters are crucial to ensuring that the mission of becoming "number one" is successful. Someone who wants to get to the top, will at the same time take a self-critical look at what they still need to do and what new skills they need to acquire in order to jump over all the obstacles that await them on the way to the top. The path to the top is clear, it is known to you, and you've got it all figured out with the appropriate intermediate stages. Reaching each stage's goal is at the same time a small interim victory, a small reward on the arduous path to the top. Without letting yourself be stopped, you move forwards with determination. The plan dictates how and where to go - and how fast. At the same time, you know that you can rely on yourself. After all, no one has ever climbed to the pinnacle of success without self-confidence. You are focused, have the goal clearly in sight and because you're sure you can do it, you're willing to take the small step backwards here and there. You don't let that stop you. The path is the goal and then, at some point, the time has come - you arrive! You have made it and have reached your goal. You are at the top, you can't get any higher. It is your moment, your triumph, and your victory podium. You made it to the summit of your success, which you always had in mind, in focus.

And now? What's next? You've achieved everything, what else is there to come? This is exactly the moment when many successful people let go in confusion - and lose their grip. For most of them, there is only one way to get off the top - and that is to fall. This happens faster and easier than many people can imagine. But why? Why doesn't someone who is at the top simply stay at the top? Psychologists are familiar with this challenge and they also know the answer: Because those who have reached the pinnacle of success suddenly no longer have a goal. What comes next? This is a question that is familiar to all those who have not yet achieved success because they usually had no goal and plan. Many successful people at the summit are therefore downright disoriented. They neither know where to go nor what to do. They want to stay on top, but they don't know how. It's almost as if they have to start over again. They've lost their inner compass and their focus.

You definitely don't want this to happen to you. You have made significant progress with the first two Pink:Code keys. You are pink and you are positive. Now you have to cherish these mental strengths like a precious gift and use them to your advantage. Keep a steady positive outlook on life. Or put differently: Once pink, always pink! Because this code of life builds itself up modularly. One part fits into the next, until it is perfect and functions one hundred percent.

The art of seeing and thinking positively is actually not an art at all. It is rather a constant in your life from now on. A fixed value and an eternal gain that always aligns to your mindset and by not "falling off the wagon." So, have you stopped watching news shows packed with bad news? Great, then don't even think about starting again. If you didn't miss the disasters of this world yesterday, you won't miss them today or tomorrow. Or do you suddenly miss the feeling of being dragged down? Are you feeling like being in a bad mood again, for self-doubt and do you want to crawl under the covers again? No? Well, then just leave it and keep the positive things in view because if you are, and remain positive throughout, you simply get more out of life. This has also been scientifically proven. Among other things, while the immune system can be burdened by the effects of negative thinking, it can also be strengthened by thinking positively. People who think positively are demonstrably less likely to feel ill, and their risk of cardiovascular disease or mental illnesses such as depression is lower than that of pessimists. Their overall quality of life is higher and, in the best-case scenario, even their life expectancy increases. All this was outlined, among other things, in recent studies in 2022 by Dr. Elise Kalokerinos and her team at the Australian University of Queensland. In 2019, as part of the study "Optimism is associated with exceptional longevity in 2 epidemiologic cohorts of men and women," a team of researchers in the School of Medicine at Boston University led by Lewina Lee, took a closer look at the health and life expectancy of pessimists and optimists.

Still have questions? Judith T. Moskowitz, professor of medical social sciences at Northwestern University Feinberg School of Medicine in Chicago, has also developed eight skills to promote positive emotions. Studies have produced clear results in this regard. Namely: They lived healthier and longer - when only three of the following eight skills were firmly anchored in their daily lives:

1. Jeden Tag ein positives Erlebnis erkennen.
2. Koste diesen Moment aus, schreibe ihn auf oder erzähle jemandem davon.
3. Beginne ein Dankbarkeitstagebuch zu schreiben.
4. Schreibe eine positive Eigenschaft von dir auf und beobachte, wie du sie einsetzt.
5. Setze dir ein erreichbares Ziel und beobachte deinen Fortschritt.
6. Schreibe etwas auf, das dir vergleichsweise wenig Stress bereitet und finde Strategien, wie du dem Ganzen etwas Positives abgewinnen kannst.
7. Erkenne und übe täglich gütige Taten.
8. Richte deine Aufmerksamkeit auf das Hier und Jetzt und nicht auf die Vergangenheit oder Zukunft.
(Source: JUDITH T. MOSKOWITZ, Professor for Medical Social Sciences)

If such a fulfilled life is not reason enough to permanently stay in positive thinking mode and, moreover, to be a true Pink:Code user, what is?

STAY ALERT - THE TINIEST MOMENTS CAN SHAPE YOUR FUTURE *Happiness*

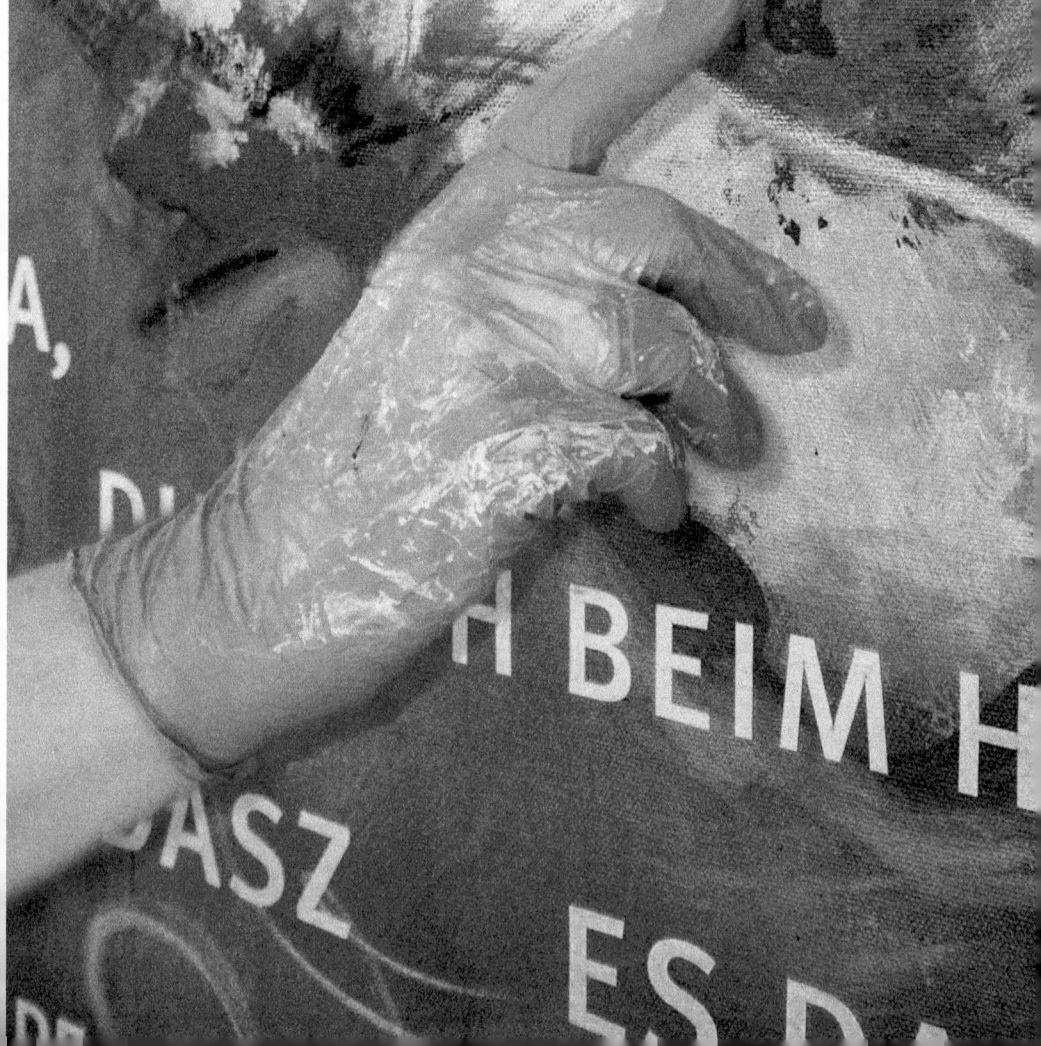

Self-liberation - the breakthrough to a new life

My heart leaps with joy and enthusiasm when I think back to that decisive moment. Even many years later, I still get such a good, indescribably pleasant feeling that motivates me. I once again become aware of how I got out of my own hamster wheel. It was the moment when I had the courage to put on the brakes instead of crashing into a mental wall with my eyes wide open. A wall that I had not built, but whose construction I had silently endured and allowed. But that was all over now. I followed my path, which led explosively through the middle of this very wall - into my own freedom. But, and this is part of the truth as well, there is no freedom without responsibility and certainly not without personal responsibility. But what does responsibility entail? Challenges that have to be accepted and that can also be unpleasant at times.

In my case, it was the trip home from Munich and the conversation I had with my parents. How would I announce my good news, which probably was not good news for my parents? My head was spinning. Thoughts were racing through my head. But I knew that I shouldn't beat around the bush. Clarity! Truth! And - no compromises! As soon as I arrived at home, I started to get down to business: "I want to discuss something important with you today after the restaurant closes, no matter how late it gets...", I announced to my parents. Now there was no turning back and somehow my parents also realized that it was an important announcement for me. When the time came, I was direct.

"As of today, I'm doing what I've actually always wanted to do and will start my studies in communication design next semester!" Boom! You can imagine that my father was anything but thrilled. On the contrary. What did that mean? How would he assess the situation and deal with it? Also in regards to the restaurant. From his point of view, he had worked hard together with my mother to build up and leave me an intact, functioning foundation for my future, and now this? The reaction of my mother, however, was different, and the first thing that came out of her lips was the exclamation: "Great!" After all, as a young adult she had wanted to live out her creative streak in the field of fashion, which in turn was forbidden by her father. She seemed all the happier that her own daughter could now escape this dilemma and that by standing her ground she could continue her journey for her own sake!

Yes, I allowed myself the freedom to follow my heart. The associated responsibility that I once again had, was of me needing to financially manage everything alone again, just as I had done in Regensburg. So, that's what I did. These new studies were my fulfillment. They were the ultimate hit and in two respects. It wasn't just the subject matter that excited me but on top of that, I was lucky enough to meet my now husband there. We quickly hit it off - both privately and professionally. Together, the two of us started our first projects together during our studies, successfully implemented them in the colorful world of advertising, and after a short time it became clear to us that after graduation, with a diploma in communication design in our pockets, we would immediately start our own business. So that's exactly what we did and our top degrees helped us do it. As we were the two best students in our class, we won our first awards before graduating, and were practically booked for work right from the graduation ceremony. Anyone who says that ability and performance don't pay off is wrong. We are the best proof! But this was not a gift, but again the result of hard, intensive, concentrated and professionally competent work at the highest level. Or as I like to say, "To wow with know-how!"

Six weeks after graduating, we founded our agency together which took off both nationally and internationally! The work did not become less, but all the more fulfilling. We put our heart and soul and passion into it - for ourselves, for success and for our future together. Germany, Switzerland, the USA - we had arrived in the big wide advertising world and felt truly at home. Regardless of whether I was studying or working on my own business, I of course helped my parents and continued to support them however and wherever I could. For me, that meant working from 8 a.m. to 6 p.m. in my own agency. Thinking, designing, planning, creating, developing ideas, implementing, pitching, customer and order acquisition and staff management. A full and also extremely demanding program that more than filled my time up during the week. But finishing work at 6 p.m. is more wishful thinking than reality. After all, working in an internationally oriented agency has more to do with "rocking around the clock" than with regular hours. And yet - after work? It wasn't the end of the day, because then it was time for me to continue helping in my parents' business. As you can see, the supposed hamster wheel increasingly mutated into a rapidly whirling giant wheel.

A screw fitted tighter than it should be can only be overtightened and will eventually damage the thread. Only in this case, I was the screw. This intense schedule and workload, went on and on for the next few years. When others took a breath, I continued to work out of dedication and loyalty to my parents. When health problems arose, I felt even more obliged. For a while, although there are only 24 hours in a day, I acted as if I could single-handedly suspend the laws of nature. Even if I varied my time commitment at the agency a bit and invested the time saved there in my parents' restaurant - it was still 16 or 18 hours of full-time action every day. If someone had introduced me to the popular term "work-life balance" back then, I would have taken it as irony or sheer mockery. Work? Yes! Life? Somehow also! Balance? Well, not really! Today I know better. But back then I was blind to myself and also in a certain way resistant to advice.

Even to my husband who saw the disaster coming more clearly than I did, I just did not listen. The first signs of total exhaustion had long since made themselves present. Sleep deprivation, sweating, exhaustion, lack of concentration and in the mornings, mounting tension in my neck resulting from the fear I had of the day ahead. Then an inner panic slowly set in. The unwanted bill for my unhealthy lifestyle, for my excessive commitment and for my self-sacrificing work effort was soon to come: More than 40 severe migraine attacks afflicted me until the summer of 2014. My health - physical and mental - was suddenly in the dumps. Yes, I knew I couldn't go on like this. Maybe you know this too: You know what to do, but you still don't do it, for whatever reason. You just can't find the right way or time and exactly this sentence, this thinking is wrong! It is a self-deception, because there is not just one suitable moment. Why not? Because every moment from the moment of realization is the right one. Now! Here and from now on! Flip the switch. You just have to do it and show the necessary consistency. Not tomorrow, today! Not later, but right now! Thinking and acting in this way is also a question of discipline, or rather self-discipline. Today I know that but at that time, I deliberately set myself up to be blind and deaf as far as this realization was concerned. Rather, I needed a reason to rethink and a tangible impulse to finally act accordingly and that's exactly what I got.

The trigger was a friend of my mothers who was a chef. Someone who always had a few extra pounds around the waist but who still saw no reason to change his lifestyle and indulgences. This was until he experienced various heart attacks – and survived. An a brutal, almost deadly wake-up call, one that he heard clearly and listened to. When he met with my parents afterwards, he was a visual sensation: He had lost over 35 kilos in the meantime and he did it the healthy way. His salvation was a metabolic cure. No more and no less. Unbelievable, but true. His impressive story would become a real life-changer for me only a short time later - even though I couldn't have known it at the time. How could I? Because we only learned that he had received this special concept from a pharmacist who lived and worked only a few towns away in Kreuzlingen. So, he applied it and his verdict was more than clear. "Since then, I've been doing just great" he said, beaming with joy.

A few days later, upon his recommendation, the pharmacist in question was sitting with my mother in our restaurant. It goes without saying that my mother's rigorous work life had taken a toll on her health. Health challenges here and there - she wasn't shy or skeptical about sharing her health challenges with the visitor. I, on the other hand, kept a low profile, stayed out of it all, and didn't even participate in the conversation.

Only a few weeks later however, I noticed how my mother had increasingly started to blossom again. She was doing very well and you could see it in her face and I especially felt it in the way she impacted me and others. In the past three to four weeks, things had really changed for the better. In my own exhausted state, an almost daring thought suddenly popped into my head: If this is good for my mother, then I guess it can't hurt me either! This is why I decided to test the products and the concept myself. After all, it could only improve from here, I thought and that's exactly what happened. After just three days, I could literally feel the energy slowly returning to me. Shortly thereafter, I was finally able to sleep again. The first time in about three years! Without nightmares tormenting me. I slept blissfully, like a baby. As happy as I was about it on the one hand, I was also very surprised on the other hand! Was it due to this concept which my mother had also used? The longer I thought about it, the clearer it became to me: Yes, it works, it helps and it is useful!

At this point however, a "but" is more than necessary: As much as the products along with the concept helped me, I did not want to leverage them to turn them into a business. Or at least that's what I thought in the first place! Network marketing? Not what I wanted! I already had two professional tasks that more than fulfilled me - the agency and my parents' business. How could I think of adding a third line of work? That would have been pure madness. Self-inflicted hara-kiri! I already had 16 hours or more on my daily to-do list, so why add even more to the list?

Actually, I was right ... But this business just kind of happened. Secretly and silently. Sounds silly but it simply just happened. And I could neither do anything about it, nor could I "protect" myself, because you just can't defend yourself against opportunities and unique situations. Fortunately! Such events just happen and sweep you away and this wave of happiness and fascination swept me away into a new, different and better life. Into the extraordinary and exciting business world of network marketing.

3rd Key: **PERSONALITY**

What a personality! – If someone says that about you, then you've pretty much made it. You're standing where you've always wanted to be - right at the top. When other people talk about someone in this appreciative way, it's like a verbal accolade, because someone who represents a role model for others is a "complete package." It is not necessarily a mere trait, a virtue or a special competence that is praised and emphasized. No, the recognition applies to the entire person - and here primarily the character, the charisma, the behavior and the way of articulating oneself counts. The visual appearance, the look and the natural appearance are secondary. Even the most expensive cosmetic surgery or beauty intervention cannot change this. A beautiful nose does not make a personality. A muscular six-pack does not create an aura, and even the best hairstyle, and the most elegant clothes are not indications of being able to act as a true personality. All these are added extras, which can at most raise and strengthen the impression a personality makes.

There are always people, who do not merely enter a party, or join a celebration, or go to an event - no, these people just literally appear and with their presence they almost cast a spell on others! They convey a mental magnetic effect, attract others like honey and the sunlight do. Because they radiate and spread an indescribable aura. No, we are not exactly in the middle of a fantasy Hollywood blockbuster here, where there are special effects and the white knight is surrounded by a radiant glow of glory. No, this previously described and depicted fascination of other people is not tangible, nor is it visible in real terms, but it is there and it can be felt by others. Because it is people who impress. People who have radiance and are a personality.

Is that a matter of luck? Is it in their genes? Are these people chosen? Are they gifted women and men? No, no and no again. You are just as much a personality as they are, but maybe you just don't know it yet. Perhaps you are still holding back your personal radiance, your effect on others, because your light is still being diminished by other things. Or you have not yet sufficiently developed, strengthened, and thus brought to light the qualities that would let you shine. Simply put: You have the switch to let your light shine brightly, but you have not yet found the button to turn it on. All of this, in fact, is a process that cannot be implemented or accomplished in one fell swoop. It is a progression and parallel development to become more and more the best version of yourself. At this point we are talking about personality development and this is much more than just having good manners and following etiquette. It's also more than mastering the few self-evident things from cleanliness and a neat appearance to kindness, compassion, and gratitude. A personality can communicate, it can listen and talk. It masters the sending and the receiving of signals. It knows how to convince, but also to withdraw at the right moment. A person with personality knows how to deal with other people. This is because such a person knows who they are, knows how to assess their behaviors correctly and the effect these have on others. One listens to such a person, values their opinion and why? Because they know how to use words as well as gestures and facial expressions. People with personality have one thing above all however: The necessary touch of humor. They are not aloof and certainly not overly serious, because it is also their smile that makes them seem so charming. Personalities are friendly, lend their ears to others, and are skilled in the art of taking a step back. Sometimes less is more. Active, conscious, listening is sometimes more valuable and more conspicuous than talking loudly. Because both convey a certainty to others: This personality has competence and know-how.

But there are other facets that give a personality an aura and these are not obvious virtues, not direct or outwardly recognizable merits. I am talking about the mindset. Such people have a firm mindset, are stable in character, have principles and above all - they live and embody these values. They stand for something, are convinced of their ideals, and know how to represent them fully. People with personality are not "pushovers", but rather women and men who stand up for what they believe in. Opportunism is a foreign word for them. Do they tell others what they want to hear in order to please them? No, not at all. They are convincing. They persuade others with their own strong conviction.

And now you will probably believe that I have painted you the picture of a superhuman with words, right? I can reassure you: Absolutely not! Because such a personality is nothing else than a completely normal human being with real grounding. On closer inspection, they are just a "normal" person, someone like you and me because all that makes up a personality, all that I have mentioned in the above sentences, is nothing extraordinary. None of these abilities and skills are things that you can't discover for yourself. Maybe they just need to come to the foreground a little more? They need to be polished and made to shine and this process is simply called "personality development." That precisely, is the way to this said, best version of yourself. Or, to stay in the vernacular of the Pink:Code, it's polishing yourself from pale pink to a shimmering, vibrant pink! One that makes you glow and that stands out. Because hardly any color is more striking than pink, hardly any color has more luminosity, more intensity and at the same time more warmth. Therefore, a key to the secret of the Pink:Code is your personality. Build your Personality! Be pink!

THE FOUR MOST IMPORTANT TRAITS, THAT DEFINE THE **PERSONALITY** KEY:

1. MINDSET – TWEAKING YOUR OWN PERSPECTIVE

In almost no other sector or industry is mindset as crucial and important as in network marketing. Here, success is not only a matter of planning, but also a matter of mindset. The right levers have to be pulled in order to do what needs to be done. If you want to make a career in this industry, you can do it, but it's not something you can just do in passing. It requires the right attitude towards the requirements and the specifics of the system. You need the right mindset, and the synapses in your brain need constant, loving, fine-tuning to keep you permanently on course. Being pink does not mean staying pink forever. This is not an automatism according to the motto: Once achieved is enough! Rather, to fulfill the positive effect of this color-state with consistency, to live it out and also to be able to enjoy it, one must be permanently prepared to work on oneself. It requires a certain readiness to question oneself again and again, to want to deal with oneself and to be self-critical. In order to keep your mindset permanently on track, you have to be willing and able to deal honestly with yourself. A laissez faire mindset has no place here. Rather, openness is required and the willingness to examine oneself over and over again. Is my inner compass still correct? Have I always consistently done what needs to be done? Where have I gone wrong in the meantime and where do I possibly need to change direction? A guiding principle in network marketing is: Check yourself daily and this slogan carries weight, because it is a call for a daily "mindset update."

You will encounter the word "mindset" just as often in the network business as in the Pink:Code. Precisely because many things are purely a matter of mindset and therefore your attitude must be right. That's because just slight deviation off the path to the goal can have fatal consequences. The decisive reason why, in the end, you miss the said target by a hair's breadth. To ensure that this doesn't happen and that the performance trend curve runs as continuously upwards as possible, the mindset must be precisely set to run like a Swiss watch.

Easier said than done! Because if you know where the dangers lurk and what can most often lead you off the right path, then that's already "half the battle." Most of the time, you fall into traps that you don't know about. In network marketing it is on the one hand the insufficient perseverance, the handling of defeats and setbacks, the lack of leadership competence and diminishing efforts after initial victories and on the other hand the false sense of security arising from it. Those who believe that they have already reached the halfway point will only ever see the goal from a distance but will never arrive! All these supposed traps and obstacles harbor the danger of shifting one's mindset. Even one small detail is enough to fail later on. So why miss out on great success when it can be so easily avoided? Therefore: Better to be and stay pink instead of casting shadows on your individual shine.

The new-fangled term "mindset" means nothing more than having the appropriate attitude towards certain tasks. It is the knowledge of how to act in the face of challenges and how to master them. Above all however, it means having the will to tackle and overcome these difficulties in the first place. Then the "mental train" is not only a little off track but is completely derailed. The right attitude is an essential necessity in network marketing. But what is "right", you may ask. Well, the right attitude is knowing what needs to be done and what is required to achieve the individual goal. Someone who is unconditionally willing to do exactly what needs to be done - and then follows through. On the other hand, someone who struggles with a wavering mindset is a person who is wavering. Because such a person is insecure, fights with and against themselves and thus slows themselves down.

But if your mindset is solid, then you are immune to nasty surprises. You then know how to assess situations and deal with them accordingly. In this respect, it is necessary to give your mindset a "broader pink." Your mindset is more than "just" having the right perspective on the challenges in the network or in the job. It goes into your character and is thus also a part of the personality development described earlier. If you don't claim to deserve only the best, you will in turn have a hard time giving your best in terms of performance. Those who don't know how to deal with failures and who don't accept that defeats are also part of success, will stand in their own way.

My recommendation to you is therefore: Take your time - and not chances! The best thing to do is to go through your personal mindset checklist every evening, which you should create in two columns. On one page collect all the mindset checks for your career.

For example:

1. Do I believe in my success?
2. Am I convinced of my actions?
3. Is my goal really my personal goal?
4. Did I do everything that needed to be done today?
5. Was I consistent enough?
6. How often did I recommend my product today?
7. Did I tell others about the opportunity of my business often enough today?
8. Do I really believe in myself?
9. Do I know my strengths? And if so, what are they?
10. Did I use my strengths completely today?

These are all closed questions that you can answer simply - but extremely honestly - with yes or no. But remember: One no is enough to cause the mindset to wobble. You need to readjust. Then there is the second column. The mindset check-up is about you personally and therefore about your personality. For example:

1. Am I strong - and what speaks for that?
2. Do I deserve success? Name three reasons for it.
3. Will I make it? If yes, then tell yourself why and what you have already done!
4. Can I handle failures? If yes, tell yourself how you do it or analyze what you want to do better and differently in the future.
5. I deserve only the best! True, but why? What makes you happy?
6. What challenges are waiting for you and why is this an opportunity for you?

You'll notice that the answers aren't the same every time, even if the questions are always the same. Because it's all in your head - today you think one way and tomorrow you think another. That's okay, because the most important mindset is that you are at peace with yourself and feel good. Because pink is beautiful and not a constraint! No one should feel good because it's an external command, but you should shine because it comes from within. Be pink on the inside, then you also shine on the outside!

2. HUMILITY AND GRATITUDE

It's easy to say thank you. So easy in fact, that it almost seems to have turned into a mere phrase. Much like the common question; "Well, how are you?" You say it without questioning it, much less knowing or rather - acknowledging - the meaning of the words contained within. You just have to put it to the test when someone greets you with the aforementioned phrase. How do you feel? Tell them honestly - especially if happiness, cheerfulness, and good mood do not seem to flow out of your pores. The expression on your counterpart's face will literally become strained if you start to list why things don't seem to be going well for you today. Let me say this right from the start: This has nothing to do with a lack of interest in you or with indifference. Not at all. I don't want to imply something like that to anyone here. But in any case, your answer would be extremely surprising if you said anything but "good". Because in truth nobody wants to have a real answer to these "meaningless expressions." It's just a polite question that people generally ask out of courtesy, not because they're genuinely interested or curious.

And what about the word "thank you?" If you're honest, it's not really any different. After all, that's what your parents taught you, to say thank you and please. Thank you, a word that is quickly said without meaning, without accentuation and without any real significance. If someone hands you something, you say thank you. In almost all actions that you do not perform yourself, but from which you participate in some way, even if it is only extremely marginal, you say thank you. Even if you don't want to. Imagine you are standing with your partner at the front door. You both have a key. Only one of you is faster and opens the door. What does the other say? Right, thank you! But please be honest - for what? For the fact that the other one was faster? For managing to put the key in the keyhole and turning it in the right direction? Not really, right? You see how quickly an important word can degenerate into a meaningless phrase?

At the same time, saying thank you is something extremely important, because saying thank you has much less to do with decency, good manners, or an adequate upbringing. That too, but what is primarily important is what we express with thanks. And that is recognition! The deed is one thing, the gratitude is another. Both belong together like Yin and Yang.

However, if thanks is missing, the deed virtually comes to nothing. Unfortunately, this makes it clear that I do not take any notice of the other person's attention, that I do not attach any importance to it. I am almost tacitly downgrading the quality of the deed and signaling to my counterpart: That was so insignificant, that it deserves no real recognition from me. If you think about the motto "Not criticism is praise enough" which prevailed in German companies for decades, you only now realise what kind of work atmosphere must have existed there.

On the other hand, the network marketing system relies on exactly the opposite: Praise and recognition! Not only because it is good for people, but rather because it expresses appreciation, motivates, produces performance, provides a good, happy feeling, and because gratitude brings people together. Gratitude creates lasting bonds! It's about shaking hands and smiling at each other. Gratitude is thus a mental fertilizer for functioning teamwork. To the point: Gratitude must express an honestly intentioned appreciation! That is, that the attention of the other, whatever it may be, is worth a thank you and thus great recognition.

Almost nothing makes us humans happier than praise! There is even a biological reason for this. Because of the way our fragile, easily shaken self-esteem is knitted, confirmation from the outside is permanently necessary. Social recognition appeals directly to the reward center in our brain, and dopamine is released. Thus, gratitude has an effect on the brain and it goes even further. The researchers Prathik Kini, Joel Wong, Sydney McInnis, Nicole Gabana and Joshua W. Brown from Indiana University in the USA wanted to know more and conducted a study: 22 out of a total of 43 participants, all of whom were in professional treatment due to depression or anxiety disorders, were asked to write a letter expressing gratitude to someone at the beginning of their therapy sessions three times a week for 20 minutes. In this letter, they expressed their gratitude to the recipient - regardless of whether they wanted to send it afterwards or not. After three months, they as well as the control group - underwent a brain scan.

The result: Compared to the control group, the 22 subjects who performed the gratitude exercise, showed significantly more activity in the brain regions that are activated by the feeling of "gratitude" - the frontal, parietal and occipital lobes - even months after the experiment. This means that gratitude is active and recognizable in the brain as an emotion in its own right. Gratitude therefore literally "rebuilds" the brain - and not just for a day or a week, but permanently. The more often and regularly you practice gratitude, the faster, more long-term as well as stronger it will be anchored in your brain and thus help you to form a new attitude towards life (source: Sciencedirect.com).

Gratitude however, does not stand alone in the Pink:Code. It has a constant companion that adds to the value of appreciation: Humility. It means understanding that nothing can be taken for granted. Maintaining this perspective is more than being grounded. It is an approach that in turn, generates honest gratitude. Anyone who still appreciates their home, their family, their job, their friends, their health, even water, sunshine, or a sincere burst of laughter, is grounded. All of this cannot be taken for granted and that's exactly what we should always keep in mind. Just pause for a few seconds in hectic, complex times and think about how quickly one thing or another can cease to be tomorrow. Suddenly, what we used to take for granted is gone. This can happen faster than we imagine and because that's the case, we should all be grateful for it.

This awareness includes two other factors. One part is respect, which is contained in humility and the other part is a close friend of humility; courage. Because it also takes a fair amount of courage to be humble and to express it. Not everyone has the courage to be appreciative, but let's be honest: Have you ever told a colleague or partner in the network today how happy you are that they are there? Have you made it clear that it is not just a given? Then say it - you will certainly be thanked for your humility, but it is also a bit brave to be sufficiently self-confident in your humility.

The Pink:Code makes it clear with its play of colors that you should shine and radiate. Absolutely. But do so without exposing yourself. That is precisely the art of it. Gratitude and humility therefore make you what the business is really about: Letting other people shine and also giving them the chance to grow, because only then will you realize what unique, great, and wonderful talents you have in your ranks. Take a step back and shine with the others. Humbly make some space so that others can step forward and for that very thing, you can be grateful. Especially when your pink begins to shine more and more brightly!

3. CHANGE & PERSONALITY DEVELOPMENT

There is an established belief that someone supposedly grows with their responsibilities. That's good! However, this also assumes that the person's personality can keep up with the growth and that they are willing to undergo corresponding development. In this case, at best, the personality is literally chasing after success. What a vivid image - almost as if Peter Pan is trying to catch his shadow again.

Anyone who studies the phenomenon of personality development will find that it is a process that never ends. The reason for this is as simple as it is obvious: Every impression, every experience, every challenge of any kind that is taken on means that you change - because you learn something new. You can imagine it like a full bookshelf. Literary works are everywhere in bound form, sometimes larger and sometimes smaller in format. But all neatly arranged. A piece of furniture full of knowledge, wisdom and experience. But if suddenly, even the smallest paperback book is added and is also placed on the shelf, both the appearance of the shelf changes and so does the content of the knowledge that this shelf embodies. It is no different with the experiences we have had in life. What you have seen, is seen. That is, was and will continue to be. You would have to switch off your complete senses and fall into a Sleeping Beauty-like permanent hibernation in order not to notice anything anymore. In short: Not feasible! In this respect, we humans are downright doomed to learn. The only question is whether we then anchor these experiences internally and process them accordingly to learn from them. That is what makes the difference. Some people put all of this in the back of their brain and never use it again. Others let their thoughts circulate around and file them under "useful, applicable experiences" in the front drawer. And the fuller this drawer becomes, the more remarkably the personality grows, thrives, and forms because it is the wealth of experiences and the skills generated from them that make up the individual.

Everyone writes their own "personal map." What they do, what they know, how confident they are and above all, what effect they have on other people. Indeed, the formation and development of personality determines the measure of charisma, which I have explained in the beginning of this chapter. Self-knowledge plays an essential and decisive role in this. It is about the same as if you were to go to school with yourself. You are everything in one person: Student, teacher, blackboard (or tablet for those younger readers of course) and textbook! In the process of developing your personality, everything revolves around you getting to know and understand yourself better. A look into your inner self will reveal a lot. Be curious! In addition, you will learn to understand why you react the way you do in certain situations and under certain circumstances. Only those who recognize and accept this, will be able to change something about themselves - if there is a need for it. Because this is also a part of development: Not changing anything if there is nothing to change but it is also necessary to be able to recognize this actual state and to evaluate it correctly. To do this, you need to find out what your goals and dreams are. How do you want to achieve them, and which principles should or can help you to achieve them? All of this is a part of self-knowledge, which is usually the best way towards further improvement.

In the Pink:Code, personality development is a bit more than just polishing up your own own self. Personal growth by using personal strengths is only one aspect. Not to be forgotten in this context is the responsibility for yourself, for your thinking, your actions, and your charisma. The most important form of responsibility is personal responsibility. Without it it doesn't work. Just as you are responsible for your life and also for your success, this also applies to your own self. It is always easy to blame others when something fails but the reality often looks different. We know this from the current judicial system. More and more often the following sentence is heard with delinquent people: "She or he had a difficult childhood...!" Maybe so! And yes, certainly these are not optimal conditions to develop into an exemplary personality but there are enough examples of people who have succeeded - despite a difficult environment, despite a not easy, beautiful childhood. Conversely, this means that it is possible! Everyone is responsible for their own pink and the intensity of color associated with it. Whoever says: "I had no choice", makes it very easy for themselves most of the time. One has a choice - almost always. Much more honest would be the statement: "I made the wrong choice!" Isn't it strange that you almost never hear this phrase? You have a choice, and therefore a responsibility, in how you deal with an experience that you've had. Discard it or apply it? Evaluate or disregard? Add it to your own repertoire or not? To let others, participate or not? You have responsibility for your decisions, because you are the helmsman of your life, you have the command over yourself and therefore you will also quickly recognize what is good for you and what isn't.

Always remember: A plant that does not grow, dies because it withers away. So, it's up to you to decide for yourself how vigorously you want to grow in terms of your personality or whether you would rather wither away. Because even your pink needs a color refresh every now and then, so that luminosity and intensity continue to shine for you inwardly and outwardly. Always be aware of this.

4. THE NEXT LEVEL: BE YOUR OWN BRAND!

Every person is unique! So are you! Isn't that great? I am always fascinated by the thought of knowing that there is only one of me in this world. Nobody is like me, and nobody is like you! We are unique and therefore something very special, something extremely valuable. Only stubborn people who are stuck in an unworldly ideology claim the opposite. They would like to make us believe that we are all the same. Nonsense! We are not! Everyone looks different and everyone has different preferences, and different needs. Everyone has other weaknesses, enjoys differently, lives differently and loves differently. The differences are infinite. It is precisely from these different characteristics that the longing for freedom arises instead of a compelling uniformity and the tendency to want to sell ourselves always and everywhere. Yes, you too are selling yourself. Maybe you just don't know it yet or haven't noticed it yourself, but you do it too. You sell yourself every day. No matter if consciously or unconsciously. Every one of us does it. One better, the other slightly less so.

It starts with your first decision of the day: Showering - yes or no? Putting on makeup - yes or no? Shaving - yes or no? For whom do you make this decision? Only for yourself? Honestly? Do you really think so? Surely you want to feel comfortable in your own skin, want to smell nice and be well-presented. You are not alone. At the latest when you step outside your front door, other people will cross your path and then the moment has come - you sell yourself. Oh yes, because you also don't want others to point their fingers at you, criticize you, maybe even exclude you. You want to be "Part of the Game." To be part of the game of life. And to achieve that, you do - admittedly perhaps unconsciously - what almost all of us do: You sell yourself! And you do it solely to please others. When you realize this, you will also realize that no one can advertise for you as well as you can. You are your best advertisement! You should always be aware of this.

Your ideal billboard sign, other than your appearance? Of course, your personality! There it is again. In the Pink:Code too, it will follow you wherever you go because you are important. Pretty much everything that happens in your life depends on you and your personality is decisive for that. But because that's the case, you are also your most important brand. Everyone knows the brand of certain sports cars, noble fashion designers or the finest perfumes. You know the name of the world-famous "lemonade from Atlanta" right away, and the name of a certain fast-food chain will be on the tip of your tongue. Why is that? Because they are brands that stand for something. You associate something with those names, something so distinctive that this brand immediately comes to mind. Well done, advertising has done a lot of things right because that's exactly the purpose of marketing and advertising. Of what? Correct! Marketing is indeed the magic word and that word is also in the name of the business, which begins with Network and ends with Marketing!

If you now realize however, that you are already selling every day and are about to become your own best brand, then I recommend to you: Play the game with full commitment! Your personality, your way of acting in business, your looks, and your way of communicating - all this should be so unique and at the same time so authentic that everyone instantly sees: This is you! That's what you stand for! This is typical for you! As a graduated communication designer, I can tell you from experience: "All this becomes your personal branding."

You embody this spirit and you live it every day, inspiring more and more people to follow in your footsteps. Because you are you and because it's great to be you! That's exactly why others want to follow you. Welcome to network marketing. That's how things work here. Now you're just wondering how to make it work, right? You want to know how to shape your own brand? Don't worry, it's not magic, but rather a matter of authenticity because if, as made clear in the paragraphs and chapters above, you've figured out who you are, what you stand for, and what others associate with you and your name, then you know what your brand is all about. Emphasize your unique qualities and all the things that make you special. Should you work with social media channels, then this profile is also your shop window now. Therefore, it is important that it also corresponds to your spirit and your intended personal branding. Once again, your personality is key! You have already scrutinized yourself and are in constant silent dialog with yourself. Great, then you also know the answers that make you appear pink. Now your third key, which is rightly called "personality", is fully developed and lies in your hand, ready for you to use to open the next lock, to get a little closer to the great secret of the Pink:Code.

IT IS NOT ABOUT WHO YOU ARE, BUT WHO YOU WANT TO BE.

BE THE *Energy*
YOU WANT IN YOUR LIFE.

One system makes it possible

Sure this business just happened. I can already see in my mind how you are all shaking your heads in disbelief and of course asking yourselves, how can one just slide into a business and without wanting it? Let me explain it to you, because years later I myself had to think about the same questions you have and become aware of what happened and how it could all have happened in the first place. To begin with let me say: The whole thing has nothing to do with magic nor does it have anything to do with the combination of certain factors. Rather, it was a logical consequence.

In the previous chapter, I told you how I felt - exhausted, tired, worn out, tormented by migraines, absolutely stressed, constantly in action and permanently in a rush, and that's exactly how I looked. Pale skin, exhausted, lackluster, poor posture and deep, dark rings under my eyes. I look as beat up as I also felt and it was precisely this appearance that I simultaneously embodied to the outside world. One that remained hidden to no one not even to me in front of the mirror. Even more striking was the difference you could see only six weeks later, after I had begun to apply the concept regularly. I felt how I began to blossom on the inside. My energy slowly but surely returned and the mere fact that I was able to sleep soundly again, and for a sufficiently long time, recharged my inner batteries bit by bit and at a healthy rate. I started the day well rested, filled with vitality and with a noticeable inner drive. A healthy complexion also returned to my skin and face and this was noticed not only by me and of course my husband but also by others full of positive surprise at the obvious change. "What happened? What have you been doing? Have you been on vacation? Did you go to the spa?" All these questions started flooding in and some even believed that a miracle had happened, because only six weeks earlier I had looked like a heap of misery. And really, it is no fairy tale, and no cosmetic gimmick - I was really restored and as such felt good. To be on the safe side, I visited my family doctor and had a blood check done and to my own surprise, my blood screening was now also showing the positive development. Something that had rarely been the case before. But this time? Everything was in perfect order and could not have been better.

It's undeniable that I knew exactly to whom I owed this state, this new well-being and healthy vitality: The concept which I initially regarded with suspicion and doubt, the one that had already helped our chef friend and my own mother to newfound energy. The question of whether I should continue to take the remedies or not was no longer relevant, as they did me more good than not and had no undesirable side effects. The medical findings showing my currently perfect blood results also spoke for themselves. No, this was not fantasy, not just mere wishful thinking and certainly not a mundane placebo effect. There was medical proof! Numbers do not lie. Here it was in black and white – no questions left unanswered!

Our guests in the restaurant were also open and refreshingly direct. They had seen me before. How I walked around looking more and more like a zombie. And now? The absolute opposite and that's exactly what they told me. They congratulated me as well as expressed admiration and the highest appreciation and of course, most of them wanted to know the secret of my newfound dynamic power. Secret? No, it was by no means a secret. In fact, I was happy to be able to share my happiness, my not so secret "secret" with others – my business that is. After all, what is good for me should also be good for others. That's how simple and direct I am. Luckily!

Without really noticing it, I was suddenly doing referral marketing and I did this for a period of around two years. I was other people's fairy godmother. I recommended and told them about everything that I had done myself. People kept asking my mom and I: "But you look great! How do you do it with all the stress in your gastronomy business? You'll have to tell me!" So that's exactly what we did. We told everyone who wanted to know why we were so fit and why we were able to be as agile as we were. As I write these sentences here, I can already feel myself raving again because the blazing fire of conviction is still burning inside of me. I can't help but talk about it. It just happens. And I found myself in the same situation back then. I simply told everyone who approached me about it and recommended these people to my later upline, the aforementioned pharmacist. Was I aware that I was actively networking? No! Absolutely not! That really wasn't even my intention. As I said: I had enough to do and was professionally completely busy. Even though I was once again filled with the necessary vitality and energy, it didn't mean that I was looking for the next or additional challenge. No thanks! I simply recommended what I did and had experienced to others. In this respect I can say today: Network? Yes! Network marketing? No! As a business, it was simply not an interesting topic to me at that time.

Honestly, to this day it is still not a business for me. It is a passion, true joy, positive automatism and for that reason, I don't see it as business because I have seen what it means to have a business, with our agency and in the parental restaurant. It is work! Work that you can feel, that leaves traces, that requires effort and exertion, where at times you have to motivate yourself. Network marketing is not at all like that, especially not if you experience and live through the Pink:Code like I do.

For me, network marketing is more than just a fascinating business, it is fulfillment and joy in life at the same time, which is a perfect way to earn money. A lot of money, but that is a by-product because the income comes more or less automatically. I claim today in the Pink:Code: The stronger, the more manifest the passion, the more attractive the income situation.

I do not know any top executive in the network industry who in some cases earns incredibly well, but complains about work, effort or stress. These things just don't fit together. That doesn't mean however, that you can become successful and financially independent without being active in the network. Not at all, but I do use the word "activity" very deliberately. It is activities driven by individual passion that generate the usually high income, but these activities are not work, because in the Pink:Code we do not feel or perceive them as such due to the existing passion. One does it automatically, simply because it is fun and it is precisely this joy that allows you to claim that you are full of fervor and conviction: I am not working, I am living my passion! That is then the final stage of the Pink:Code!

But this level of mindset is a journey. It cannot be achieved without effort, without commitment, without personal development, without progress, without openness and this aspect requires time, which you have to give yourself. That is part of the truth. Passion is not something that can be achieved with the mere snap of your fingers. You will know exactly when the time has come. Just as I have felt it. And especially when you feel like you're reaching your limits, that's when it's time to unlock the door to a new level - with the next of the eight keys from the Pink:Code.

For me, it was that time again in the summer of 2016. I had once again reached my limits. This is also a typical symptom for network marketing, that you reach your personal limits. It is precisely then, that you are once again open to change. Open to take the step to get to the next level. You open the next door with the respective key - and then it happens. It's magic! Your antennas go up, you start searching for something new. If you are attentive in this moment, if you recognize the signs, you can let it happen. That is the magic of development and individual progress! My limit was not only the workload, but also an inner dissatisfaction. I had scaled back my commitment to the agency and was devoting about sixty percent of my capacity to the restaurant. At the same time, however, I became increasingly aware that I was only using ten percent of my actual potential. In a sense overwhelmed by being underutilized.

I was annoyed, dissatisfied with myself and my mood tended towards frustration. It's exactly this kind of negative emotional feeling that weighs down on and burdens the body and mind. I vented about this exact situation in depth and without reservation with the pharmacist, who was, after all, my savvy contact when it came to recommendations. "You always think of the welfare of others. Don't you think it's finally time to think of yourself?" she told me without mincing words. A statement and at the same time a question with great personal impact and consequence for me because at that moment I found myself in the situation I had just described. I was standing on a threshold, in the midst of a moment in which I needed to open a new door for myself - to a new level. Crucial to this, was the perspective she made clear to me in one sentence: "Here in network marketing you can use and live out your complete potential - to your benefit and the benefit of others!" This conversation flipped a switch in me. One that was just waiting to be called upon, used and applied. At the same time, I had been aware for a long time that this network marketing business, from which I had always closed myself for the aforementioned reasons, had much more to offer me than anything I had ever done before. Especially since I had already been doing it anyway due to my large number of recommendations in the previous two years - without wanting to do it in the actual sense. I knew deep down that the freedom and individual development opportunities that I had been wanting for for such a long time, were waiting for me here.

Now it was time to be honest with myself. To admit to myself that I was perhaps not on the wrong path but had reached the end of my previous path and that it was now time to take a turn and leave at the next exit. Last exit "network marketing business." I was ready for what I didn't want before but this realization was also a process and a result of self-reflection. The crucial question was: Do I leave everything as it is and continue like this for the next few years or do I change something? If so, what am I changing? Why is it important for me to change something? What are the consequences of this supposed change? All questions to which I quickly had a clear answer and that alone was enough of a sign to take the exit. A huge opportunity was opening in front of me that promised me improvement through change.

SELF-REFLECTION - BE HONEST WITH YOURSELF!!

A brief reflection is not enough. Anyone who questions themselves must also be uncompromisingly honest with themselves. No sweet-talking or excuses, are helpful here. As a practical tip for you: Self-reflection should always take place in the morning and evening. It's best to do it as a small ritual shortly before getting up and then before going to bed.

The basic questions to answer are:

- What are my goals? Where do I want to go? Where do I want to arrive? The goal MUST be clearly defined, otherwise there is the danger of missing the intended goal.

- Am I currently already on the right path to get there??

- What do I have to change in myself or in my circumstances?

- What can I influence? What can't I influence? Because only things that I can influence myself can be changed by me. Things that are not in my own hands are therefore things that I do not have to actively address because I cannot change anything about them despite my efforts. It would therefore be a waste of time and energy.

YOU SHOULD ASK YOURSELF EVERY MORNING:

1. Why am I getting up? Why do I choose to be active today?

2. What is my goal today? What do I want to achieve today? What will I do in order to get noticeably closer to my goal again today?

YOU SHOULD ASK YOURSELF EVERY NIGHT:

1. Which daily goals did I achieve and which did I not?

2. Did I really do my best today to achieve my intended goals?

3. Where could I have increased my efforts even more?

4. Why did I achieve the goal? Or what did I do wrong so that I did not reach it?

Consider the following aspects for further reflection:

- Do I think positively in all matters? Have I found or at least set my focus
on the positive?

- What can I specifically do to improve a negative or stressful situation for me??

- Is there someone who can support or help me? Important: Never be afraid to accept help. Nothing gets better just because you try to master something on your own.

- Write down your learnings, your insights and the knowledge gained. What can you take away from them? Writing them down is helpful to overcome other challenges or to avoid repeating mistakes!

Remember: making mistakes is not a problem. We all make mistakes. But: We should learn from them and therefore not repeat them!

4th Key: **PROMOTION**

Those who do not show what they've got, cannot hope to be discovered and those who do not speak cannot be heard. You consider these findings to be self-evident and obvious, right? You may even be correct but one thing is for sure: Exactly these mistakes are made again and again. Many entrepreneurs and self-employed individuals lack clear visibility. An unfortunate situation. Because put simply: How then can a customer base be built and sustained? How is someone supposed to desire something or develop a need for something if they don't even know, that something that they could need exists? Doesn't make any sense, does it? As a comparison, I would like to give you the following example: Imagine you want to open a store and sell health products of the best quality. Yes, you are truly convinced of the quality of your products. You have done your research, compared the suppliers and the ingredients. You have looked all over the world to offer only the best of the best to your future customers, because you have a mission with your new business: You want to make the world a little bit better than it is and finally make sure that your customers really do eat healthier. You only want to do them good and, in turn, earn money, which is more than legitimate. You have good intentions. So, what needs to be done? What's next? Okay, you've found a store, you've made it look nice because you want your customers to feel at home. You've even come up with a sensational name, so that even passing shoppers will notice you from the outside. Above all, there's something else you've managed to do: Despite the current shortage of skilled workers, you've already found someone who supports your idea and wants to help you out in the store. Then the time has finally come. Opening day! You unlock the doors to your store. Everything is ready - including you. All that's missing now are the customers who will storm into your store and buy everything. Enough goods are available, the warehouses are full, everything is nicely displayed, decorated, and arranged but strangely, no one comes. All day long your store remains empty. Not even one customer comes in. But you don't mope about it. Tomorrow is another day and what's the saying? "With a new day comes a new chance!" But: No one has ever generated success and good sales with just chance. Too bad that your store remains empty for the next few days. Damn it, don't people want to be healthy? Don't they know of your good intentions?

Well observed - finally! No, that's exactly what they don't know. How could they! You have forgotten the most important thing because of your misplaced humility: Promotion! You didn't draw attention to yourself, to your business, to your products, to your good intentions and to your ideas. This is a mistake that can cost you your entire business. Because there are very few things are more important than getting out there and spreading the "good news" that you're there! It is important for self-employed people and entrepreneurs to shout loudly from the rooftops "I'm here, and, where are you?" Even the best business idea is useless if no one knows about it. Promotion is a critical business tool - and an essential part of the Pink:Code. You can be as positive as you like, think, and act pink and have the right personality but if nobody knows you, the business is doomed to failure.

Attract attention instead of holding back! Your business information should be accessible to everyone and everything. Always remember the slogan: "Listen to my message! Because what I have to tell you is of interest to everyone - including you! Me and my info are therefore important and valuable to you!" Is that too much for you? No, it certainly isn't. Be open and honest, authentic, and communicate with vigor and strength. This is not a case of "less is more." On the contrary, in the field of promotion, the motto is "It can't be bulky and flashy enough!" The point is to attract attention. Being present is the top priority and the first business obligation - always and everywhere. Those who voluntarily hunker down in the basement do not have to hope for daylight and sunshine. If you want to experience the light, you have to step out of the shadows and the darkness. And that's easier nowadays than ever before.

As a graduate in communication design, I can still clearly remember the high-quality campaigns that my husband and I developed and published together in our agency for other companies. We developed new corporate identities, our own color schemes, typographies and new slogans. One play on words followed by the next. Always having an idea and implementing it according to a client's specifications. Don't worry, you don't need all that. Especially not in network marketing because there is one thing that is primarily in the foreground: Your authenticity. Just make use of your existing keys in the Pink:Code first. Show everyone else how open-minded and positive you are. That usually infects others enough and makes them curious. Because most people are not that positive and pink, so with that, you already stand out. You can be sure of that. And if you also score points with your amazing personality, then you can be sure that it will definitely work.

How do you do that? Through honesty and with your conviction. There are plenty of ways to be effective on social media channels. Create a Facebook profile for you and your business, make yourself visible on Instagram, or reach a young, dynamic, and open-minded audience via TikTok and these are just a few of the many social channels. This is where you show off who you are and what you've got. Connect with other people around the world. And most importantly, let everyone you've already made "happy" with your idea, business or products tell others about their positive experiences. Post all of that on your channels. You can then be pretty sure that your happy customers will be heard, seen and accordingly noticed with resonance. This is promotion of the smart and clever kind. Show off your pink and take advantage of the eye-catching nature of this great color. You are completely different. You shine and shimmer with all your keys out of the Pink:Code - like a flamingo in pink! Now you have gotten there, are present, are your best promotion and therefore are more pink than ever before!

THE FOUR MOST IMPORTANT FEATURES THAT DEFINE THE **PROMOTION** KEY:

1. ACTION – BECOME VISIBLE AND MAKE IT HAPPEN

Never before has dedication, commitment and targeted activity been so valuable and necessary as it is today. The infamous network phrase "Get out of your comfort zone!" is hardly more justified than at this point. You have to do it, you have to be active and you have to make sure that people notice you. Others cannot do this for you or can only do it to a very small extent. Here you are challenged. It is your turn! You need to be aware of this time and time again.

Why again and again? Because constant energy is required for this important commitment. Have you ever heard the clever phrase: Nothing becomes old as quickly as news that was just reported? You've read it, understood it and put it in the far corner of your mind. Put simply, this means that a reel or a post, e.g. on Instagram, fizzles out so quickly in the recipient's mind that there can be no question of a lasting effect. Of course, this raises the question of whether the activities on various social media channels are useful at all. Oh yes, they are! But only if you "stay tuned" over and over again. These channels have to be used daily so that you can achieve a constant level of attention from your followers and then maintain it. Believe me: I have done it myself and the effect or the successes from this activity did not take long to come.

And that is already the next important keyword: Consistency! It is an essential component of visibility. Otherwise, you would quickly fall into the typical "out of sight, out of mind" behavior. Especially nowadays when we are all virtually inundated with news, info, and impressions. Wherever you go and stand, your smartphone is with you and with it, its many apps, the Internet, messenger services, social media, chats etc. All of this is available to us in abundance today. For some, it is a kind of curse, for others a blessing and that's exactly how you should see it: Your chance to become visible. But again, the same applies here: You just have to do it!

But how to increase visibility when you're in danger of getting lost in the shuffle? Let's be honest: How much useless, superfluous and really even low-level stuff is there to see? And even worse: Who posts such "intellectual garbage" in the first place? But that's exactly where the challenge, the art and the real task lie. Specifically, to fight against this flood of superfluous stuff and to stand out, to become visible, to make a name for yourself. And that's not really that difficult if you know what makes your followers tick and what the wider user community that you want to win over and convince is like. Because what do they eagerly look forward to? That's right - variety and good entertainment. Yes, that's the truth. People want to be entertained more and more these days. Even with news and information. Not dry, not matter-of-fact, but they prefer to experience and consume one thrill after another. Hence, it should be clear to you: Give them exactly what they want and achieve more visibility through quality infotainment, because that's the ideal mix. You fill a cocktail shaker with info and entertainment and what comes out after shaking it? Yep, perfect infotainment posts!

I can already anticipate how you might be wondering and asking yourself now, how and just what do you do about it. I know, not everyone is an advertising expert, a filmmaker and not everyone is bubbling over with creativity. It's easy to say someone should be creative, but it's far from that simple. There's much more to it than that. In this respect, first ask yourself: What do you like about yourself? For example, what did you notice while looking through the Instagram app and what "stuck" with you? What can you remember? That's a good parameter to help you get your bearings because what you spontaneously remember, is also what you kind of liked or impressed you in some way. Just act accordingly. Especially in the beginning it will make your first steps in becoming visible easier if you fall back on already existing ideas.

Believe me, with time you will become more and more confident yourself and at this stage your own ideas will come out more and more because once you know how it works, your security will increase. And with confidence comes ingenuity. You inevitably become more creative because you come up with more and more. I have experienced this firsthand myself.

When it comes to the "how" of making your messages visible, it's important not to overdo it - neither in what you say, nor in how you look. Stay true to yourself. Because if you're playing the clown when everyone else out there knows that you're just not a natural-born solo entertainer, (which wouldn't be a bad thing) then you shouldn't pretend to be either. Adorning yourself with other people's feathers has never led to anything. Rather, make sure you keep your high standards and bring your personality into it.

After all, that's what stands out and catches the eye: Class! That means: Colorful? Yes! Colorful and confusing? No. Better a bright pink than a confusing color explosion! Pay attention to your wording and only say what you really want to say. Avoid foreign terms and slang - they often don't go down well and are not easy to understand for everyone. Simple, clear sentences are much more impactful than lengthy videos of sweet nothings. I can promise you: People will tune out and your message will fizzle into nothing. Instead, say clearly and concisely what great things you have to offer. Straight to the point and without embellishments. It's much more honest and it's much more you! I could also say at this point: **This is pink and not baby pink!**

2. COMMUNICATION – A CORE ELEMENT IN PINK

Whether with words, gestures, facial expressions, with your outward appearance - no matter what you do or don't do, you are constantly sending out signals. You cannot protect yourself from this. Hence the basic theorem in communication science: You can't not communicate! Every look can contain an intended or unintended message. Every movement, every facial expression, the way you walk, sit, and even how you dress or wear your hair. Everything is communication and that makes communication probably the most important phenomenon between us humans. We exchange information, ask others to do something specific, take note of something, react to something, or cause others to do or not do something specific. Of course, we also usually expect a reaction to our own signals. Communication is therefore based on reciprocity where communication partners interact with each other. The bottom line is that communication is something great because it triggers activity and a response in the form of action. It is exactly this knowledge that gives you an excellent chance to put yourself in the limelight in an appropriately targeted manner.

Communication is at the same time an essential component in the network marketing business. This fascinating business thrives on people exchanging information, interacting, informing each other, and passing on recommendations. "Have you heard...?" or "I absolutely have to tell you about this...!" would be typical opening sentences to tell others about the products or the business model and give it a sense of urgency or necessity. Because the Pink:Code is also primarily about talking about yourself and letting people talk about you. Yes, you are the center of attention here. Don't worry, that's not arrogant or a bad move to get attention. On the contrary, it is important to attract attention and to use it positively: For yourself, for your cause and for your mission. After all, you have something to offer, you have something to say - information that only serves its purpose when it is shared and passed on to others. You should always keep this in mind.

If you live by the Pink:Code, you need to not only demonstrate who you are, what you have to offer, and what your message is about, but you also need to communicate intentionally. After all, it's completely different whether you showcase your success or brag about it. Do you consider these to be the same things? Then let me take this opportunity to explain the difference to you. Bragging about your success would be an exclusive reference to yourself. You glorify yourself and at the same time make it clear that in a way only you are responsible for this status and that you have achieved it only because of your own unique skills. In summary, this message says only one thing: No one is as good as me - and certainly not you! Such miscommunication excludes, repels and is extremely unlikeable.

The other way to talk about yourself and your success is the empathetic, sympathetic way. It invites, it lets you extend your arms and sends your recipients the message: "What I can do, you can do too. Yes, I'm proud of what I've accomplished but it's not a unique art that only I can do. You can do it too and the great thing is, I'm happy to help you do it!" Someone who demonstrates his or her successes in this way, who shares, rather than glorifies them, makes themselves a people magnet. Because someone like this attracts others in an extremely friendly way because: Success is and remains sexy! Success is likeable! Success is the expression of being able to achieve goals. Success is proof that you are making progress in life and it is something that in one way or the other almost everyone would like to have. When you reveal yourself and tell others about your experiences, you become the best example of your own statements. You emphasize and substantiate your own credibility. Your communication is the real and figurative statement: "Look, it works! It works! And I invite you to try it yourself. You can be sure, because I've proven to you that it will benefit you, do you good, and help you and others get ahead in life!"

And that's not all. This form of communication can even be intensified considerably: That is through others and their confirmation! Testimonials were once invented for this purpose. Originally, this was understood to be a very specific type of advertising in which well-known personalities recommend a product and advertise it. The purpose of this is that some potential customers consider these celebrities to be more credible because of their name recognition. In network marketing however, the concept of testimonials is applied somewhat more broadly and wisely. Let's be honest: Whether it's a well-known actress, an athlete or a celebrity from any other field, does that just mean I have to believe everything they say? You can safely have your doubts. Just because someone is good at kicking a ball doesn't necessarily mean they are credible in other areas. The same applies if someone plays Hamlet brilliantly, sings Mozart's Magic Flute or authentically mimes a mafia boss in a film. All well and good, but does that make someone credible and trustworthy?

It is different when someone recommends something who has had their own experience with it and now shares it with you. That is highly credible because someone like that, earns a certain amount of trust. They can give you assurance as to whether something is effective, works, is good for you or does you harm. Someone like that can warn against or recommend. In this respect, there is hardly anything more useful than many, many authentic recommendations of this kind. These are testimonials that have a great impact, because they contain content. In this respect, I can only encourage you to collect all such feedback and share it with as many other people as possible. They are meaningful and have an impact - and they are honest and convincing. Demonstrate the benefit so that this in turn benefits you and your commitment!

If you want to be pink, then you have the courage and even the joy to present yourself with your radiance. However, the fact that you always feel comfortable in your own skin always requires one thing: Honesty! You are what you say, and you do what you think! The testimonials of others help you to consolidate your status. At the same time, they spark a certain level of curiosity. Along the lines of: "If he also says that, there must be something to it...!" And the effect is even better if it reads: "What she can do, I can do too...!" Testimonials from other users are proof and a motivator in one. They confirm and challenge at the same time. This is typical communication - reciprocal, targeted and informative. But it also open, honest, pure, and powerful - completely and utterly pink!

3. UNIQUE AUTHENTICITY

The quality of actors is pretty easy to judge: The more they are able to embody the character of their role genuinely, the more impressive their acting performance. So, what's our verdict then? "Wow, that was really authentic!" There we have the word which this chapter will revolve around: Authenticity. Some define it as a kind of congruence of inside and out. Others talk about character, behavior, and mindset having to be in harmony with each other. To me, this sounds rather paradoxical, something like "It has to be black to be black!" Black is black - this color, unlike pink, cannot be increased in intensity because a little less black and it becomes gray. But do we ever add a little more black to the black? No, because nothing would actually happen. And the same applies to authenticity. It is all or nothing. There's no such thing as "a little bit authentic" - you're not a little bit pregnant, a little bit dead, or a little bit alive. One is alive or not alive. One is authentic or one is not. In this respect, the definition is not as complicated as some might think. Whoever is authentic is credible, genuine and their actions correspond to their character. Someone who preaches water and drinks wine is anything but authentic.

What does this insight mean for you in network marketing and especially as part of the Pink:Code key of "Promotion?" Only if you are authentic, you are also credible to others. Because only in this case will other people listen to you, pay attention to you and in the best case emulate you. Always remember: Your message is too important not to be credible! You can improve the lives of many people and change them for the better. You can make the visions, hopes and dreams of others come true. You are a true distributor of opportunity. On one premise: You have to be credible
and therefore, also authentic.

Authenticity is also a question of trust. It means: You don't hide behind a false mask, but show who and what you are and that's more important than ever these days. Because in times of an increasing flood of fake news, of photos whose original subjects have been edited to such an extent that there is hardly anything left of the original, where misinformation is deliberately spread for whatever reason, your credibility and your level of trust is something very special. It is a valuable asset with which you can work and at the same time the perfect bonding medium between you and other people. Anyone who is to rely on you must be able to trust you. They must be able to rely on your authenticity.

To reach this stage, which is not difficult, it is first and foremost a matter of only promising what you can deliver. Those who exaggerate will reap above all, one main thing: Many disappointed people. Authenticity is one of the highest forms of honesty and this also includes admitting what you can do - and what you can't do (yet)! If you know that your product can do a certain thing, then share that with others. However, you don't have to overdo it and attribute umpteen other positive effects to your product. As the German saying goes, "He who lies once is not believed. He who lies twice is never believed again!" In other words: Someone like that has lost his authenticity forever. That would be a shame, wouldn't it? It doesn't have to be! Who wants to trade in their beautiful, bright pink for a faded, meaningless color?

Especially since authenticity doesn't just affect you alone. It also affects your downline. Because your team also stands for something - for your good values and thus also for your credibility, for your trust, for your honesty and for your conviction through authenticity! The area of promotion therefore always addresses both parts - you and the team. That means: You promote yourself as well as your upline and if you take a close look at the word, you will notice that there are two significant syllables hidden in it, both of which stand for themselves and each of which has a meaning. The first word is "pro" and the second word is "motion." "Pro" means "for" and can be interpreted in a personal sense, such as being there for someone, supporting them, actively participating and caring for them. It expresses a certain nuance of caring that can be crucial in a professional setting. It is of utmost importance to be authentic when leading a team, promoting a team's mission, and advocating for a team's success. The second word, "motion", represents feelings, motivations, and inner intentions. It defines the team's character. As the leader of the team, your actions will have a dominant impact on the team's mental state and situation. This is what promotion is about - projecting emotions towards something and conveying the effects of those emotions in a meaningful and sustainable way. This is what you do with your pink personality and thus also with your entire downline, which is shaped accordingly by you and your authentic leadership. Together you are the pink climbers who can't be stopped and who give their promotion a great deal of expressiveness through cleverness, authenticity, creativity, and visibility. This Pink:Code key opens a huge door to a world where communication can make a big difference - all you have to do is apply the key and open the lock with it.

4. RECOGNITION IS VALUABLE

As I have just told you about consistency and continuity, there is another essential part to perfect promotion. Something that really underlines the consistency of what you do and that is the value of recognition. How many slogans from advertising have managed to become almost an integral part of our daily lives? Surely you can think of a few. You simply must admit that advertising is effective and those who came up with it really did do a good job. Often it is enough for someone to say only the first words and another person can complete the sentence right away, because this slogan has almost burned itself almost already into their memory. And again, and again, you also think of the corresponding product, even if this doesn't play any role at all in the acute context. Does it seem strange to you? It doesn't have to - because there is something behind it that you should definitely take advantage of in your business. You should acquire a certain recognition value and by reading this book right now, you are already on a really good path to achieving that. Because with the Pink:Code you embody a color that is not common. That alone has a fair amount of recognition.

Of course, any message, whatever its form and nature, will be recognized more quickly if it is repeated over and over again. A certain reliable continuity coupled with a high number of hits is not everything. Just imagine a company logo. One that you know, that is famous and that you can clearly see in your mind. Sit back, close your eyes, and draw the logo from memory. It is not difficult. You know the shape, the type of letters or characters and, above all, you know the color that belongs to this well-known logo. Now try to change only the coloration. Maybe the logo you imagine is blue, now imagine it in orange, and again in purple. Do you realize how difficult it is to imagine this alone? It starts to bother you right away because you secretly know that there is something wrong. It just doesn't feel right because you know this corporate logo in its origin. It has become firmly and clearly embedded in your mind. That's how you've seen it multiple times - always in the original and always unchanged and there is a reason for that. Because this always unchanged presence underpins the recognition value tremendously. You recognize the company behind it. You don't have to look very closely or even for a long time, because you know immediately what it is. But even more - because with the immediate recognition of the logo, you also associate the values of the company, what it stands for, just as quickly as the name. You immediately have one or even more products in mind and maybe a jingle, a commercial or a slogan comes to your mind. All this determines the value of recognition.

But now I ask you: Do you already have this recognition? Are you already so pink that everyone knows right away who they are dealing with? Is your message so striking and so permanently consistent that people immediately recognize you, your business and what you have to offer? Or are you already drawing attention to yourself with constant regularity, but people still don't immediately know who you are? I already have an inkling as to why that is: You meant too well with your posts, your visibility. Always trying to bring variety into everything? Always different shapes, always different colors and always different slogans? Here's where the lack of recognition comes in.

What you need is a system, combined with a uniform appearance. This is your look for success! Get your style! Just look at someone else's Instagram account. With all those colorful pictures, looks and reels, would you recognize them right away? I'm sure you wouldn't. The reason for this is as simple as it is obvious: all these posts and reels lack a consistent look and appearance. Because only this, combined with a frequent number of hits and a continuous permanence, provides the necessary and equally important recognition value. One click, one look - and you know who it is or what it's about and that doesn't just apply to Instagram. There's a reason why successful companies and equally successful products appear in the same scheme over and over again: They want to be instantly recognizable. That's all. And it works. So, all I can do is give you some pink advice as a professional communication designer: Do the same and create your recognition value.

Again, you don't have to conjure up explosions of color, shapes, and graphic design. Just decide on a single pattern. Perhaps from a post with where you have triggered a particularly large number of reactions because that alone is already an indication that you were on the right track here. Leverage the experience wisely and duplicate your success with a new message, but in the previous style and apply it repeatedly. Your channels get a much tidier appearance, the clarity is increased, people recognize you faster, immediately connect images with you, with your business and with your portfolio. Or you can use special apps where you can easily create smart video messages. In this way, you create your look, your form of communication, you are always up to date and generate a terrific recognition style for yourself that makes a real professional impression. And if you're really clever, you can use the recognition you've created throughout your team. Thereby, the entire downline also works in this uniform form and external presentation. The outcome: Your recognition literally goes viral.

Of course, if you're pink or have your own particular style, then you'll stand out, you'll attract attention, but if your whole team is pink, it's a mass demonstration of intensity that simply can't be topped. Because: Unity through uniformity makes you unique! Then "un-stop-able" becomes pure "un-top-able!" Therein lies the fourth key of the Pink:Code, complete and firmly in your hand!

YOU HAVE UNLIMITED POTENTIAL - DEVELOP YOURSELF FURTHER.

POSTING IS LIKE PEEING — KEEP IT FLOWING

DO THE *Best*
YOU CAN WHERE YOU ARE,
WITH WHAT YOU HAVE.

New thinking, new luck

My decision was: I'm in! I'm taking this opportunity and giving myself one year to do it. My challenge in doing so was how to integrate the opportunity into my daily routine. Planning was half the battle and I knew that it could be done. It's the will and the planning that counts. For anyone who tells me today that they don't have time to improve their life, I smile at them and confidently point to myself. I am living proof that the bogus argument "I don't have time" is not a valid argument. Because for yourself, for your own future and for a better life, you always have time – everyone does!

You have to make time. For me, this resolution meant getting up an hour earlier and that in turn meant having one hour more per day at my disposal. And that's an activity you can do too! I used this one extra hour for my new business. In addition, I carefully analyzed my restaurant commitments and subsequently knew that between peak hours there was an opportunity to schedule another hour or two for the new challenge of network marketing. Why was this planning important? To get consistency into the business. To establish a system that created a reliable regularity in the day, and within my own rhythm. Of course, a certain amount of discipline is required. But no profession is possible without it. For me, this is a critical base for success. Those who stand on the ladder but don't have the discipline to do what is necessary and climb up to the next step, will never get ahead. Rather, such a person will permanently remain in one place. In this respect, the subject of discipline is not a topic of discussion for me. It is a basic requirement in everyday professional life. That is a fact!

My perspective on the new venture was: Time! To gain more time for myself. I had a certain amount of faith in myself, my potential and the new system. My calculation was quite simple: If I invest more time at the beginning, I will receive a higher return later! One could also say with a dash of irony: I planned to earn some more time with even more work. At first glance, this sounds more like madness than logic and yet, it was precisely this equation that worked in my favor. Because what did my balance sheet look like so far? Sobering! I had neither more income, nor more time, and certainly no vacation. What was I working so hard for, please? It was precisely here that I was sure that the result of a time investment in network marketing, would turn out considerably more positive and thus in my favor.

So much for the theory! And the practice? To undertake something is only one side of the coin. On the other side is the concrete implementation of the plan. For me, this meant doing things differently than before because I knew that even if I saved a bit of time elsewhere, I still didn't have the necessary freedom that others had. I was more or less forced to make other arrangements. For example, I didn't have the time available to conduct one consulting or sponsoring meeting after the next on a daily basis. I decided to bundle the necessary activities. From a purely intuitive point of view, this was probably a wise decision, because it allowed me to save an enormous amount of time while being extremely effective and efficient. So, I did this by using a side room in our restaurant, inviting many candidates at once to a specific appointment, and having my trusted pharmacist, who was now my upline, give the appropriate talk during the initial period. Efficiency with ideal job sharing - it could hardly be more efficient. My power - her professional know-how. It was a perfect fit! So perfect that we achieved dream quotas in no time at all as the candidates more or less all registered with us as future partners. At the time, we had a completion rate of over ninety percent - these were results with a wow effect. I also left the on-boarding process to my upline, because I simply didn't have the time for these administrative things but it worked and better than I could have ever dreamed of in the beginning.

Until one day she called me and congratulated me from the bottom of her heart. "Great job! Congratulations! You've reached the next level of sales!" - "Excuse me? What did I get?", I asked, completely dumbfounded. Honestly, I had absolutely no idea about the career plan. So, when she told me that about 800 Euros would arrive in my account in the next few days, it was all over for me. Completely confused, my first reaction was: "Oh God, I'll have to call our tax advisor first...!"

To all of you who are holding this book in your hands right now and smiling: If you have this kind of reaction in such a situation, just because you receive "gains" in your account, then you have really done something right. Even if it's only unconsciously. For me as a former student of business administration with an intermediate diploma however, it was like an initial spark. Because at the same moment I knew what I had to do: Study the career plan, and study it in depth! So, what did I do? I contacted our head office and had everything explained and pointed out to me down to the smallest detail and in the process, I became more and more aware of the unbelievable, sensational opportunities that were waiting for me. I almost got into a real gold-digging mood. Especially because concepts like passive income, measurability and transparency in action and the associated income opportunities became obvious. Good that I asked so persistently and really wanted to know everything, because only then did it become clear what enormous potential there was in this network marketing system in every respect.

Another key experience was an event of my partner company, which I attended shortly thereafter. The atmosphere there was impressive, contagious, and magical at the same time. I could hardly believe it. Especially when I discovered what great careers had been created and admired there. "Can this be true?", I kept asking myself, almost in disbelief, rubbing my eyes in amazement. I had never experienced anything like this before. What these good-humored, cheerful people there earned and how they for the most part lived their lives with dedication and enjoyment was more than amazing to me. Above all, they all seemed to have what I missed so much: Time!

One question increasingly thrust itself upon me during and also after the event: Do I really have to be this old before realizing that an opportunity actually exists for me to utilize all of my talents, skills, and potential? Yes, there is! And with this realization, I really got started. In doing so, I relied on the digital path, especially in the beginning, by significantly increasing my visibility via social media. I made it simple and also trusted my upline. Facebook, Instagram & Co - I covered the entire repertoire on the social web. Every day a post, week after week and with absolute continuity. The reward was not too far off. People outside were increasingly aware of who I was, what I do and what positive message I have for them. A solution that can be an answer to the problems of many others! My message was as simple as it was effective. Since I was in a phase of change myself, I also shared my own experiences. A topic that has an inherent spirit, which in turn touches others. They felt addressed and heard. The decisive factor here: One's own authenticity. With all my openness, I was also extremely credible.

At first when I claimed that it was not me who came to the job, but the business came to me, it is also because network marketing possesses an imaginary power through fascination. It is a system that has exactly the answers to certain questions, desires and needs in life that many people have in mind. The only thing is that you don't get these said answers in conventional working life. Why not? Because they don't even seem possible or real behind a previously hidden horizon. Anyone who is employed in a company, no matter in what position, or who as a self-employed person exposes themself to the daily struggle for customers and sales, can hardly believe that passive income exists at all. For them, freedom and independence, self-determination and free time management are so far away, more a sense of utopia than vision, that they believe such a thing simply doesn't exist. Therefore, I encourage all networkers more urgently at this point: Go out and tell your story! Show and prove to other people that they all have the chance to determine the course of their lives freely and on their own. Yes, there is this great opportunity. It is not a fairytale, even though it may sound downright fabulous at times. Network marketing is reality, it is real, it is tangible and above all it is a considerably more serious business than many other businesses. In this respect, my statement at the beginning is also true: Network marketing just happened in my life. Especially since my path to it was not only atypical, not even a hint classical. I basically inspired myself out of ignorance, recruited myself, sponsored myself and trained myself and all of this without even really wanting to do it. It happened because I let it happen. Yes, I probably brought in one or the other competence and other quality and this was without really noticing it or without intentionally using these virtues. However, I had a deep longing: I wanted to somehow get off my previous, rapidly whirling hamster wheel, the curious paradox however was that: At first, I wanted to get into this hamster wheel at all costs.

I deliberately gave up my business studies to study communication design. I completed this demanding course of study with enthusiasm to found and run a successful agency, which I also succeeded in doing together with my husband. In other words, I was determined to do the job that came with it. In addition, I agreed with full awareness to help my parents with their business and to take on a great deal of responsibility there as well. No one forced me to do it; I did it all voluntarily. Summing up, I can say today: I willingly entered the hamster wheel! Up to the time, when I felt that I had reached my limits and was in the "red zone." I wanted to get out! And the exit I found madly burdened me with even more work and on a terrain that was completely unknown to me. One that I neither knew nor really understood from the beginning. It was there where I first became involved with an indefinable kind of enthusiasm and conviction, although I had nothing of it myself. More health! More income! More freedom! And as if that wasn't crazy enough, I unconsciously did this job almost perfectly. Until someone from the outside came along and gave me the long overdue wake-up call by asking me to get involved in a system that was new to me. I agreed to this, again knowing that I only had a small window of time available, which was really too small for the industry. At first glance, this looked like complete madness and it didn't stop there because I consistently took advantage of the time I had. The result: I grew my downline faster - and without really noticing it. In addition, I also earned money, which I also didn't really have in the back of my mind. To be honest: I didn't have a plan! That's why I made myself self-sufficient and being smart I got all the info that was even remotely necessary. That was the moment where I became aware for the first time that something had changed. Had I arrived? No, but I was in the middle of my journey, I had set out and was on my way to something completely new. To something that was promising. Which was also the solution to many of my questions and the salvation for most of my hopes. Above all, I was finally in the middle of getting off that hamster wheel that was holding me back.

An exit that took place step by step. At the beginning of 2017, I managed to double sales with my team. What conclusions did I draw from this? First: It works! Despite the agency! Despite my parents' business! And that, in turn, generated an extremely decisive realization: If doubling sales is feasible under these circumstances, what would be possible if I concentrated one hundred percent on my new "self-liberation business?" And another key realization came over me like an epiphany: I had noticed that I could finally develop and use my complete potential in this new business! I had finally found a path where I even had the opportunity to be able and allowed to grow past myself. Nothing and no one were limiting me. What a blessing! This awareness alone made me mentally grow wings, but this enlightening realization alone was not enough. In contrast, there was still the agency and the restaurant. My experience in the network showed me that I was limited in what I could achieve in my other jobs, despite additional work and increased commitment. Here I would always come up against some kind of limitations. Limitations that simply do not exist in network marketing.

From this realization I also drew the next conclusions: I had to reduce my time investment for everything that was not related to my new business. At the same time, I had to set myself a concrete goal. One that was proportional to the reduced commitment. I put my focus and energy on reaching a certain career level. I knew with the decision I made what the consequences would be. That was, if it worked out - and I had no doubt that I was not going to make it - I would close the restaurant, which I was now solely responsible for, and reduce my involvement in the agency to the bare minimum. I went through what was a liberating, albeit arduous thought and development process, made only possible through the many insights gained through network marketing and its achieved results. It became clear to me in a self-reflection, what I really wanted and what goals I wanted to achieve at the end of my journey. Along with a clear motto: Now it's my turn! For years I was there for others and was always giving to them and put my needs on the back burner. But now my time had come, and I was finally thinking of myself. Why? Because I had earned it!

5th Key: **POWER**

In the long run, only power helps! Even though the whole world seems to be talking about deceleration, work-life balance, taking a break, pausing for a moment, and reducing stress. Honestly? There's nothing to be said against that because the word "power" in no way contradicts any of these concepts. Rather, it's about doing everything you do right for your own success, for your career, for the fulfillment of your hopes, your dreams, and your vision. In this context, it means that you do all of that with enthusiasm, concentration, commitment, and dedication and above all with joy! Because if you drive with one foot constantly on the brake, you shouldn't be surprised if your progress is slowed down. If you then also take unnecessary breaks in between, this not only costs time, but also nerves and your own motivation increasingly falls by the wayside. What many people don't know: If you take it too easy, are too relaxed, and comfortable, you will certainly lose track of your goal and in a way be shooting yourself in the foot. After all, we humans are wired to arrive as quickly as possible with the greatest effectiveness and efficiency and to implement a plan in its entirety. It is in our biological disposition to sprint instead of being permanently and endlessly on the road like a marathon runner - both psychologically and physically. That is why it is important to go "with power." Focused and committed, we define the goal and manage the distance to get there. This way of proceeding is innate to us. Maybe you know the phenomenon that time just seems to stand still when you are bored. Maybe you have even experienced this in your professional life. You've done everything, you've completed all the tasks you've been given, and from that point on there's nothing left to do today. You look at the clock. There is still some time left until it is finally the end of the work day. But what now? There is nothing left to do and only a little later you look at the clock again. Time seems to stand still. In fact, only a few minutes have passed and yet you feel as if you've been waiting for an eternity. Another example, which may be just as familiar to you: You are on your way to meet someone but a quick look at your watch which indicates that: You are way too early and will reach your destination much sooner than expected - and most importantly earlier than necessary. The time you plan to waste does not seem to be going down and it seems like forever, until it is finally time for your meeting ...

The feeling is completely different when you are actively engaged or enthusiastically occupied with something. When you want to create or achieve something in a certain period of time. I can reassure you: Time runs at the same pace in both situations. A second remains a second. Nobody turns the clock but still, the minutes seem to fly by. Because you are busy, you're active, and you're powering through - engaged, focused, and concentrated and there is also another important factor: Everything that brings you enjoyment and fills you with joy, is time well spent. You let it spur you on internally, and at the same time the deceptive feeling arises that time has once again passed more quickly. Because fun somehow never lasts long, weariness and monotony, on the other hand seem to last forever. But there's a reason for that, and it applies specifically to the fifth key in the Pink:Code - power! Five American researchers initiated a study on this apparent phenomenon and their hypothesis was the following: If time passes faster than expected, it is perceived as more exciting and positive in retrospect. If, on the other hand, it passes more slowly, it was supposed, that it was perceived to be dragging and dull. To test this theory, the researchers had participants read a text and underline all words that contained a double consonant. It is fair to say that this was a rather boring and dull task. The highlight of the study: The participants were told that the task would take exactly ten minutes.

And here it comes: Half of the participants were interrupted after only five minutes and told misleadingly, that the ten minutes were already up. On the other hand, the other half of the participants, were only stopped after twenty minutes. To no surprise: The first group accordingly had the feeling that the time flew by quickly, while the second group had the feeling that time was only dragging on. Just as the researchers had expected, participants in the first group reported a significantly higher level of enjoyment, challenge, engagement, and fun in completing the task than the participants in the second group. The same findings were confirmed when the researchers asked both groups to work on on the task for exactly the same amount of time (ten minutes) but were simply told that the task took five and twenty minutes respectively. The results were the same regardless of whether the groups were asked to underline words or do other tasks such as listen to music. So, why do people judge an activity to be more exciting when they feel that time has passed quickly? Or again, why do people feel that time passes more quickly when their activity is supposedly interesting and more fun? On the one hand, because they are looking for a reason to have an experience that is surprising to them. People love that positive element of surprise. If they feel that time went faster or slower than they expected, they will wonder why that is. The obvious explanation is that the activity they were engrossed in was particularly exciting or boring. In fact, in another study, the researchers found that the activity was rated as more or less exciting and fun only when the indication of the elapsed time was surprising.

Quelle: Sackett, A. M., Nelson, L. D., Meyvis, T., Converse, B. A. & Sackett, A. L. (Source: Sackett, A. M., Nelson, L. D., Meyvis, T., Converse, B. A. & Sackett, A. L. (2009). You're having fun when time flies: The hedonic consequences of subjective time progression. Psychological Science, 20.

Honestly, is there anything that speaks against power in achieving one's own visions? This is "pure pink!" Because if you go to work with power, then you automatically need less time for it and thus shorten the distance to your goal. In addition, you will enjoy it much more and your motivation level will be much higher. So, you benefit from the fifth Pink:Code key in many ways and so does your team, because nothing is more infectious in activities than the joy of doing and a high level of motivation. Therefore, make yourself aware every day: Power is pink and pink is power! I recommend that you write down this great insight in big, bold letters, print it out and hang it up where you can see it all the time and very often!

THE FOUR MOST IMPORTANT FEATURES THAT DEFINE THE KEY: **POWER**

1. THE VALUE OF RELIABILITY

Nowadays, it seems like everything is expected to be taken lightly.

"Relax and take it easy. Don't be so pedantic. Stay cool and calm. It doesn't matter...!" If you follow these guiding principles on vacation, you're doing everything right but when it comes to your career and your success, probably not. Or do you believe that it doesn't matter, when, and if you achieve your dreams? If so, and please be honest with yourself, then you should also seriously ask yourself whether the dreams you have, are really your own dreams. Whether they really represent your deepest desires and spark an intense feeling, an irrepressible longing inside of you. Because only if this is the case, then they are important. I recommend visualizing your dreams to make them more tangible. How? It's easy: Take a magazine or surf the web and look for photos that represent your dreams - the material as well as the spiritual ones. Whether it's your dream car, the mansion of your dreams, a trip, or your longing for freedom, for love, for influence, for success. Cut out or print the pictures and stick them on a large piece of cardboard. I can promise you, nothing works more than creating a collage or so called "mood-board." One with your own hopes and dreams. This will make your goals much clearer and your desire for them much stronger, because in the end it's about your own fulfilled life. Your life's dream, your personal enjoyment and your joy in life. So are you going to let a misguided social mantra take that away from you? No way! Just give yourself a break and take it easy! It's about you and your future happy life. That's not something you should approach with a loose and relaxed attitude. You only have one life and time is limited! So stay focused, stay on it - with power.

All of that is exactly what makes you a bit more authentic, reliable, and responsible. Yes, you heard me right - these are precisely the qualities that "power-like" commitment brings to the implementation of a challenge. What good is it to rave about your dreams, tell others about them, and revel in colorful images. That's just fantasy and tends towards being unrealistic and utopian. But if you are serious about your life's dreams, you act accordingly and that is exactly what others see in you. Someone who does what needs to be done because they are honest and remain true to themselves. At this point I can only advise you to always say what you will really do later, what you will put into practice. Anyone who only utters empty phrases, who uses empty words and who does not base their actions on their words is simply a phony and therefore untrustworthy. You won't be able to rely on someone like that. No team would follow someone like that. This can only happen when reliability and the acceptance of one's own responsibility are obvious. The question of how is very easy to answer. By not only being and remaining true to yourself, but also by only demanding of others what you expect of yourself. That is pink! Bright pink! Everything else is nothing but an opaque color gradient.

Reliability starts with punctuality. If you're invited to a meeting, you can't be ten minutes late. Anyone who offers to help, but then always finds excuses for allegedly not having time right now, is unreliable. That is why reliability is one of the most important virtues. Not only for your fellow teammates, but in general, it is good to know that you will fulfill the tasks you take over. It also makes things easier for yourself.

In the Pink:Code, reliability is made up of five essential subtopics that you should keep in mind.

1. Always keep your promises!
The motto must be: "Walk the talk!" If this feeling is present, there is

no need to draw up a contract on every occasion; instead, the good old handshake can come into play. Unfortunately, it has gone completely out of fashion to seal an agreement with a "handshake." Even more valuable are those people who still live by this principle and keep promises they have made verbally - without writing them down. We can rely on and trust such people.

2. Punctuality is not an embellishment!
How can you quickly and easily find out whether someone is reliable? A clear signal of this is punctuality. Or at least a timely call if you can't keep an agreed appointment. It can happen. Although I love the saying: The art of punctuality is not to leave on time, but to arrive on time!

3. Deliver – earlier than needed!
If you want to stand out from the crowd, because people in the Pink:Code are not mainstreamers, as you know by now, then show you can deliver even before the agreed time. Surprise! And what a totally positive surprise this will be! This will really amaze others - especially in your team. Unfortunately, this is no longer the norm in this day and age when everything is done at the last minute – and usually too late.

4. More than delivering: commitment!
Try to make a full commitment and you'll see it has a different effect than a mere offhand promise. In other words, before you make any commitments, think carefully about the following:

- Do I want to do this at all?
- Can I do it?
- Do I have the time?

And some advice:
Write down the time you need to complete the task in your journal and also note the agreed deadline - always two days in advance! Because a commitment is about everything and this is a commitment with an absolute "implementation-fulfillment guarantee."

5. Meeting preparation
Sounds self-evident, but how often have you been in a situation where it was very apparent that this had not happened? Therefore, once again back to the Pink appeal: Always prepare for appointments! It saves time, sometimes also money, if everyone knows what you want and what the goal of the meeting should be, because then a result will be achieved faster. This only works however, if you prepare for the meeting. It also gives you a higher sense of security because you are behind the steering wheel and not being led into the unknown!

These are five aspects that document and promote reliability and which, as you will have noticed, do not represent any real effort and certainly no real challenge. But if you internalize them and put them into practice, you are not relaxed, easy and cool - no, someone like that is "hotter than hell! Be pink! Think pink! Act pink!

2. TRUST IS UNIQUE

Reliability without trust? No, that doesn't work! But what exactly is trust anyway and why is it so important for you - especially in network marketing? This quality primarily determines your general tendency to rely on another person's word, promise, statement, or action. How much do you believe this other person? And let me say this right away: You can only really trust someone if you believe them one hundred percent. Because how are you supposed to just "trust" someone else? How does that work? Does it mean that I believe them sometimes, sometimes not at all, and sometimes only a little bit? What kind of trust would that be? Correct, none. It would be uncertainty, which would have absolutely nothing to do with trust. In this respect, the following statement can be derived: The more your trust grows, the more positively you look into the future because trust gives you safety, security, protection, closeness, reliability, openness, carefree attitude, optimism, faith, confidence, light-heartedness and a generally good feeling about something.

Trust, however, is a learned behavior that can lead back to your childhood. Our confidence stems from two core components:

1. self-confidence, i.e. confidence in one's own abilities, and
2. trust in other people.

One could also say...**trust is a learned decision!**

People who trust, assume willingly and confidently that a thing develops in such a way as promised or hoped for. Whether or not this will happen is, of course, another matter. What is remarkable, however, is that the higher a person's intelligence quotient, the more trusting they are. This is not just an assertion but has been scientifically proven because this is the result of a study conducted by Oxford University. Of course, this does not mean "blind trust", rather, the scientists assume that high intelligence correlates with better knowledge of human nature. In other words, smart people know how to assess others better and are therefore more likely to know whom they can trust and whom they cannot. And this fact even has financial implications: When Jeffrey Butler, Paola Giuliano and Luigi Guiso from the University of California in Los Angeles conducted research on trust, they discovered that people who trust a lot, earn up to twenty percent more than those who distrust a lot. Too much blind trust was however, also not good for their wallet: When the test subjects were asked to rate their trust on a scale of 0 to 10, the highest earners were found to be at a level 8. Those above this level earned an average of seven percent less.

However, because trust first has to prove itself, i.e. generally "grow," it cannot be forced or even accelerated externally. It is not an instant product, but a maturing process. At the same time, this means that trusting one another has consequences. This includes, above all, renouncing all the little dirty tricks and dodges that some people like to use or even prefer when they want to make a career for themselves. But they absolutely do not build trust:

- Showing off at the expense of others
- Concealing your own shortcomings,
- Whitewashing tasks,
- Forging secret alliances and following hidden agendas
- Exploiting weaknesses in colleagues as well as team partners

The question then arises, if trust is so crucially important, how can it be generated or built up in the first place, especially since reliability alone is apparently not enough. Is it possible to simply acquire trust, or do we have to work hard to earn it? According to the motto: "I trust you, so you can trust me." The latter sounds rather naive and could also be negligent. Often, demanding trust on the job is just an empty platitude that sounds good and somehow makes you sympathetic but is never implemented. The fact is: trust is an expression of an intact relationship - in private as well as on the job. But you can already tell from the passive formulation that trust cannot simply be commanded. It is something that is earned and for this, it needs the following five basic rules.

1. Nothing creates and maintains trust as much as talking to each other regularly and openly. Communication is a must!
2. Always say what you mean, believe, feel and do only what you say. This is the basic principle of authenticity and therefore trustworthiness.
3. Of course, you can't always speak from your heart and sometimes it is better to remain silent or to hold back. Therefore, the rule applies: Simply say quite honestly: "I can't talk about that -not yet."
4. If you approach mistakes with openness and honesty, you create a great deal of trust for yourself. Particularly if you are or want to be a good leader, then prove that it is not a disgrace to make mistakes - not learning from them is! Therefore, ideally, let others share in your learning successes! That is pink! That is generous! That is reliable!
5. Even Rome wasn't built in a day. The same applies to trust. It cannot be built from one day to the next. It also needs a test at some point to strengthen the bond.

And these following pink behaviors strengthen and promote trust in you even more:

- Openness to suggestions and differing opinions.
- Honesty about your own intentions.
- Interest in other people and their professional and personal problems.
- An open and fearless culture of conversation in meetings
- Generosity in sharing knowledge and contacts.
- Making promises - and keeping them.
- A culture of criticism that transforms ideas of all kinds into learning processes.

Trust is a precious commodity that must be valued, treated gently and carefully. Pink and trust have something in common: both are like paper - once crumpled, they will never be quite as smooth and perfect as they once were!

3. THAT LITTLE BIT MORE: COMMITMENT

Who hasn't dreamed of being like someone else? To simply slip into the skin of another person who perhaps has just that thing that you would like to have or who is standing exactly where you would also like to be. And then find yourself asking: How did someone like that manage to do that? How did they become that, how did they achieve that? The answer is no mystery at all. All these people were active. They worked for it. It doesn't matter whether they have achieved outstanding results in the field of sport, whether they were extremely successful in their careers, or whether they lead a life that one would only too gladly want to lead themselves.

But working for it alone is usually not enough, because these people, whom you would like to emulate, all have something in common. They have not only done what is necessary with a large portion of consistency but they've done a little bit more, gone that extra mile. They were all prepared to do more than just what was simply necessary. Commitment. These people have gone beyond the imaginary limit, perhaps completely exhausting their limits and possibilities.

Because those who work with commitment put their heart and soul into it. Being committed means showing full dedication. With energy. With enthusiasm. The task to which you dedicate yourself then becomes a matter of the heart, because it is precisely this extra effort that ultimately leads to even better results - and thus to the top. There is one catch however: Commitment cannot be prescribed. Commitment is based on voluntariness, but it usually makes the small, but subtle and decisive difference.

In the network marketing context, commitment describes the personal dedication and desire to give one's best and to work hard. This cannot be achieved if one only commits half-heartedly. If you're committed, you go above and beyond the call of duty, make a special effort to achieve something, and are prepared to put up with all the effort that this entails. Thus, engagement is the exact opposite of passivity and indifference. One cannot be engaged and at the same time do nothing, or be indifferent to the outcome of the activity.

Therefore, genuine engagement results primarily from two causes: Ambition and conviction. It is ambition that drives one to achieve a goal. Usually one already has the result in mind, which creates an immense driving force. This inner drive to reach the destination, to achieve what one has set out to do, or even more, is known as ambition.

The second component, which is deep inner conviction, reflects the knowledge of being on the right path and, above all, of being committed to the correspondingly right goal. One feels that the effort is worthwhile or that it will be extremely meaningful to be that "committed." This is because one is convinced that everything that will be achieved with such effort, will also give one an equally deep satisfaction, a feeling of happiness as well as a kind of liberation.

The question is: How strong is your pink commitment? Are you full of drive and zest for action, or do you tend to fool yourself and get sidetracked quickly? I have a quick little test for you that can give you some more information about the intensity of your commitment. Tick only what really corresponds to your attitude and where you can wholeheartedly agree:

❑ I find a lot of fun in my work and look forward to it.
❑ I feel committed to my work.
❑ I have high expectations of my own work and performance.
❑ In all challenges, I always try to achieve the best result.
❑ I have often been praised or even rewarded for my efforts.
❑ If required, I voluntarily do more than is necessary.

- ❑ I am frustrated by colleagues who only do what is necessary or who are too quick to settle for half of the results.
- ❑ I want more responsibility and even like to take on new challenges.
- ❑ If I notice that others are not contributing or not contributing enough, I always try to motivate them and help them along.
- ❑ It's important to me personally that my job makes a difference.

Results to the engagement test:

✔ If you agreed less than five times, it's almost a matter of luck that you took this test at all. Your commitment still has a lot of room for improvement. It's not pink yet, it's just barely pink. I really hope that this book will help you to change your attitude for the better.

✔ You agreed six to eight times and ticked things off the list? Well, that's a decent figure, but certainly not ideal. There's still room for improvement. You've basically made a good effort though.

✔ Did you agree nine or ten times? Wow! Your commitment has reached a peak value. You're a real role model! Great! Because you seem to always be fully involved everywhere. Your commitment is great and just as persistent. I'm keeping my fingers crossed that you achieve all your goals - you really deserve it. You're really glowing pink already!

And even if it's not quite enough - more is always possible. Even for you! Maybe you just need to raise your expectations a little higher or have more confidence in yourself. Because if they are high enough and you show the corresponding commitment, then you can't help but commit to yourself accordingly. Therefore: Set your goals ambitiously enough. Even if only to meet your own expectations, put in more effort and make the necessary commitment to others. That is the answer to the how. I'm sure it will work for you, too. The reward will follow instantaneously: You will be happy with yourself - and with your Pink status!

And another good piece of Pink advice: act according to the phrase: "No sooner said than done!" Because being ambitious doesn't just mean doing a lot or having lofty, but also achievable goals. Time is just as important. That means: Be fast in the implementation! Don't dilly-dally, and don't take too long to implement. As I said, everything has to be realistic, but take a close look at your goal and ask yourself if they are perhaps also achievable in, say, four days instead of a week? Remember: Saving time has many advantages. Be it more free time or the chance to start earlier on a new project with the challenge of a new goal. And there is something to the saying "time is money" after all. I could also say: Time is pink! Commitment certainly is.

4. TEAMBUILDING: EXPANSION & CONSOLIDATION

The Pink:Code radiates from you to others, from the individual to the group, from the singular leader to the Power Pink Team! Because that's exactly what it's made for, and the network marketing system even more so. Nothing against lone wolves, but their skills and strengths are only really unleashed when a whole team accepts and implements them. Because what you can do, is a cause for success in the team and creates an effect that is larger, more impressive, longer-lasting and thus pinker!

One of the biggest secrets to success in the network industry, is the emphasis placed on teams and team building. The system thrives on it. After all, that's what makes this industry so unique. It's not one person doing the work, it's many people doing what the work that is required to become successful. Have you ever tried to lift a tree trunk by yourself? Quite likely an impossible task. But as a team? That's more likely to work! Another example is the power and distribution of effort in tug-of-war, where an individual stands no chance against a united team. It's clear that the team has a significant advantage over an individual person.

Teambuilding in the Pink:Code is less about the process of getting someone excited about the business and presenting them with the opportunity. I can assume you do this with power, enthusiasm and excitement. After all, that's as much a part of network marketing as cream is on a cake. But what then? If, for example, you sign up ten new partners and then do nothing else, how many of those ten would start the business on their own? What do you think - realistically? Right, with a bit of luck probably two at most. The question is what happens to the other eight? The answer is sad, but true: they quit again, and they hadn't even really started. What a waste. On one hand, you've wasted your time trying to inspire them to join the industry. On the other hand, you've robbed yourself and them of a great opportunity to truly learn about the business and take off to become successful. Always remember: The next partner can change everything in your business. You never know what kind of human network marketing diamond you have found. But why is it that around eighty percent of all people who sign up, quit right away, before they even get started?

⇨   Because they earn nothing.
⇨   Because they don't know what to do.
⇨   Because they have the wrong expectations of the business.
⇨   Because they have been left alone.

And the last point is both the most common and the worst reason of all, because you could have stopped this very cessation - by caring and taking responsibility for these people, by helping to "pink them up." You have to turn them into pink shining people. Real pink lighthouses! How? By teaching them the basics of the business and proving first and foremost that it works. And there's a simple and proven way to do that: Show them how to get their first earnings through referrals because with the first success, with the first sale, with the first payout, the bond results from conviction! Quick success potentiates the belief in the functionality of the industry! Such a person will be loyal to you and your team will be involved and active with commitment. Such a person has their own dreams and wants to achieve them. You help them to do so - with talks, with training, with advice and action, with demonstrations, and with perfect team spirit. You are the guiding force to the Pink:Code, because at this moment you have almost all the necessary keys in your hand to open the appropriate locks for your team members. You just have to show them which doors to open and which key fits where!

Attract new partners and introduce them to the business professionally - and make them successful as quickly as possible by giving them a "taste of income in the new system." That's the perfect first step towards expansion. But unfortunately, that's not the end of it because the team still consists of loose, individually encapsulated and separated particles - the newly added, freshly on-boarded new networkers. It is not yet a team, but rather a loose collection of individualists and ambitious lone wolves. What's missing is the team spirit, the mental glue that really holds a team like this together. Through this bond, everyone works towards a common goal, instead of drifting apart in all directions. It's about bringing the newcomers and the already experienced networkers together until they are closely connected.

How? It works best with meetings, events, knowledge-exchanges, or camps, because people love company. Together is always more popular and better than alone! Thus, pink executives know that following major events held by the respective partner company, where thousands of partners of this company meet, everyone returns highly motivated and enthusiastic. What they can do, I can do too! There you go, the best motivation you can imagine. Everyone who is bright pink and therefore clever makes their own meetings accordingly. Anything else would be grossly negligent! If you keep getting your team partners together at regular intervals - once a week or at least every two weeks - and bring them to the "motivation filling station", then they will receive inspiration, empowerment and training from you and the team. This is how you become a functioning, intact, united team that works towards big goals. Because then you are no longer pink by yourself, but your whole team will shine brightly in this wonderful color. You may already be a leader but with the said actions and activities you will develop more and more into a team builder. In this way, you create a very special spirit in addition to the loyal cohesion - the Pink Spirit, which carries power in itself. This is how you keep the "mood thermometer" very high and remember: Being a little crazy never hurts because it lets you be powerfully pink and that in turn is a positive catapult for your success!

MAGIC MOMENTS, TEAM POWER AND SPECIAL EVENTS PROMOTE THE PINK-SPIRIT.

THAT IS HOW TRUE LEADERS CREATE THE FUTURE GENERATION OF LEADERSHIP.

THE BIGGEST CHALLENGE IS BEING *Honest* WITH YOURSELF.

From idea consumer to entrepreneur

What a moment! In 2018, after fifty years of success, I closed my parents' restaurant, which I had bought from them several years earlier! I remember showing them a check that, in the end, was crucial to everything that followed. "Look at this!" I said. "There's another way...!" I said that not to show off, but to make the comparison between the two businesses clear – the exhausting restaurant and the joyful business of network marketing. ",In 20 years of being self-employed, I've never made so much money with so much joy...But now I do - while having fun, with great people in my team, with terrific managers and within a sensational system!" My father recognized this too and said just one sentence: "Close the deal! Just close the deal!" This said to me by none other than a wonderful man who had worked hard all his life, who never had a single job that was too much for him, and who put in every ounce of his strength and effort into his business every day. This was something he had passed on to me, not only out of pride for his own work, but also because he considered it a foundation for me. The insight gained from both time-consuming jobs - hospitality and agency - was that time is precious and cannot be reversed.

I finished up at the restaurant and with that, closed a chapter in my life. I was now ready for a new success story - mine! Today I know it was one of the best decisions of my life. Everything has its time, and I look back without resentment or melancholy, but with gratitude, pride, and relief. Because finally there was an end to the temporal, mental and emotional pressure. I had lifted a heavy burden off my shoulders and since I was also able to take part in a wonderful incentive trip with my new partner company due to my top performance, I also celebrated a premiere: Three weeks of vacation over Christmas in one go! Unbelievable, but true! I had never been able to experience anything like that before. How could I? And during these wonderful, carefree days, I received a few more success stories. It was then that I knew that I had made it! I had arrived. I was finally where I belonged - in a business that fulfilled me. Network Marketing was my much longed-for vocation! And it still is today!

IMPORTANT INFO FOR YOU - GOOD TO KNOW:

Please remember and make yourself aware of it every day: Only one person in your life is responsible for you changing everything you want to change. And only one person is also responsible for you being able to lead the life you want to lead: And **that is YOU!** Use your talents, because you have them, just like everybody has them.

You decide whether you participate in the game of life and whether you also win. You alone decide where, when and how you engage yourself, but remember: If you decide to be there and participate, then give your best every day. With fun, with joy and with all your heart! Be yourself! Because you alone provide for your happiness, for your satisfaction. Stop making others responsible for it. Take responsibility - for yourself, for your life, for your work.

However, dreaming of a career, wishing for a career, and even getting the big break of a career opportunity - that's only one part of the picture. The other part, is about recognizing that opportunity to begin with and seizing it with both hands. Using this chance to really be proactive in order to create a career and to shape it successfully.

There's a well-known saying in German that translates as: No pain, no gain - and no action, no glory! That's the way it is. You can't have one without the other. It's good, that personal commitment has never been a foreign word for me, but rather a habitual mode. An attitude that I had learned and that my parents had thankfully taught me. This combined with enormous intrinsic motivation is an almost unbeatable combination. My individual driving force, my attraction to it, was on the one hand my own positive experiences and the enthusiastic reactions of all those to whom I had pitched the concept and which I had so far recommended to my current downline. "From enthusiastic product user to motivated business developer" - this is a well-known maxim in the network marketing industry. That's right, because I am the best proof. Your own enthusiasm is valuable and at the same time important because it is honest and authentic, and you can't achieve anything without authenticity. If you pretend, you won't be able to inspire other people sufficiently and sustainably. Because eventually the mask will fall off and at the latest then, will you reach the limits of your success. Only honesty persuades and builds trust. This said honesty was the embodiment of my motivation. The engine that drove me: I simply wanted to help other people because it just made me feel good and on top of that gave me joy. It's great, isn't it, when someone comes up to you and is happy, thanking you from the bottom of their heart just because you gave them some advice or a helpful product tip? And that's supposed to be considered work? Recommending something sensationally good to others? No, that has nothing to do with work, effort or even overcoming anything. Not at all! Especially for someone like me, who was used to real "back-breaking work" and also "mental effort."

The art of it, if it should be an art at all, is that you basically just do it to begin with. But that's not all if you want to build up a business for your own product. In addition to "doing it," there's another important aspect: you then have to do it continuously instead of just sporadically every now and then. That is the linchpin. Regularity is defined by constant practice and improvement of one's own skills. These active factors also create predictability. After a while I know what results from my activities. That, in turn, is a constant component that I can't achieve if I'm only active occasionally.

**My 1st starter bonus advice for you:
BE ACTIVE REGULARLY!**

Be active! Do it as often as possible, but above all continuously! If you take a close look at the name of the business, you will of course notice that it consists of two names: Network and Marketing. This is absolutely justified, because both parts belong together in terms of content, because the business is defined exactly by this. It is important to know: One does not work without the other. Networking alone does not generate any countable business. However, the field of marketing will atrophy if it does not meet a potent network. However, the term "network" comes first. Rightly so! After all, you do your marketing with the existing network. This means: First the network must be present, it must be activated, perhaps also reactivated because where and how do you want to "market" something without a network? Of course, I was ideally positioned in this respect from the beginning. On the one hand, people knew me in my city and in our regional area. On the other hand, many guests came to me every day through my gastronomic business, and I got to know them in this way as well. And, as I mentioned earlier, I also made myself visible on social media and that was very crucial for me and for a successful start in my business. In this way, I activated contacts, revitalized old ones, and created new ones at the same time. None of this is witchcraft, but simply the product of one's own activity. Anyone can do that – especially you! In any case, I have always been someone who sought, nurtured and cared for contacts. A virtue that was now going to benefit me more than ever before. After all, my existing network was an ideal launch pad for me.

Oh, you don't have a broad network? And now you think that's why you can't start and run network marketing successfully? If that's what you think, then you can also rejoice because I have good news for you: You either have a network or you make a network! The rule is as simple as that! If you have one, you expand it, if you don't have one, you build it up! Because having a personal circle of acquaintances - regardless of size - is not a gift from heaven, but a result of social responsibility and social activity. And if your circle of acquaintances is too small or too narrow, then go out and get to know others. Fortunately, network marketing also supports you in doing this. You get to make new acquaintances, maybe even new friends. Isn't that great? The thought of that alone excites me right now. Where else but in network marketing do you have the opportunity to do that and get nothing out of it except a lot of benefits?

From that moment on, the next phase of activity is ignited: Doing! With continuity! Now it is time to announce the good news in the personal network! There is no need to think long and hard about it. No, just do it. Close your eyes and go. Who has never raved about something? About a movie, a streaming series, a restaurant, a lipstick, a recipe, a vacation destination, whatever - surely everyone has done it. Probably every week, if not more often. And why do you do it? Because you want to share your enthusiasm with others. You want to do something good for them. Yes, you even secretly want to convince them to try it out for themselves. Everyone loves the confirmation of one's own recommendation or statement. That is completely legitimate. Honestly, isn't it obvious to rave about the product that your network marketing is all about? And to top it all off, I could see the positive effect. I was thus my best self-advertisement! I infected others with my fire. I know that sounds a bit corny, but it hits the nail on the head. And because I was so "on fire", I just did and did and did. Honestly, without really thinking about it.

I simply recommended without thinking. It wasn't necessary. Why should I have done that? It would have only slowed me down. What thoughts would have come to me in such a case? Did I address enough people? Will I be able to fill the room with people?! What should I tell them? How should I present? Will they buy my story? How should I tell my story...? Suddenly the merry-go-round in my head wouldn't stop spinning. The sobering result? You slow down yourself and hinder your own activities. You even take the momentum away from yourself, stop your own enthusiasm because you suddenly begin to question yourself and your actions. A fatal error. Who would do that when on their way to work in the morning? Imagine a bus driver starting to ponder whether his route really makes sense or whether if it wouldn't infact be better to take a different route...madness! Nobody does that. So why start in network marketing to "dislocate" your own thoughts and to "break" your own drive? Especially since you are doing nothing else than giving good, honest, and useful advice. Advice from which both parties can only reap benefits such as help, improvement of a certain condition and perhaps more income or even a new career. And one is supposed to think about that?

My 2nd starter bonus advice for you:
DON'T THINK ABOUT IT, JUST DO IT!

Brain off, activity on - if you take off like that, success comes almost by itself. Of course, the phrase "success can be planned" is true and in network marketing it is even more justified. But first the fuse of the so-called success rocket needs to be ignited in the initial phase. Once this has been done, the next step is detailed planning. And by "ignition" I mean giving everything without holding back and being active. This is what I have done. After all, we all know: What works once, works twice. I could also say: If it worked for me, it will work for you. That is a law of nature. I can also promise you one thing right now: Once you've started, once you've really gotten into the phase of actively doing something, you won't want to stop. You will almost inevitably become "unstoppable!" Hardly anyone can slow you down or even slow you down at this stage.

Why? Because on the one hand your own enthusiasm will carry you like a gentle wave, which is a wonderful feeling! This joy of creation causes your brain to release more endorphins - these are happiness hormones. I enjoy it over and over again. But also, the business of network marketing sends out impulses everywhere, which permanently provides new inspiration, new power and new great emotions. This business is characterized by fun and joy. At the time, I could hardly believe the positive whirlwind of emotions I was mentally experiencing. I had never experienced so many dazzling impressions, so much pleasure, delight, and joy all at once before. No matter if I was at my first event or on my first incentive trip. The fun didn't stop at all. I was finally able to take a deep, carefree breath, to let go and enjoy myself. I experienced the lightness of just being without feeling pressure from the outside. It was as if a weight had been taken off my shoulders.

Just as critical is reflected enthusiasm. The joy of others, which is just as infectious. This desire, this joy of success, this inner and outer jubilation of your colleagues, all this is more than pure motivation. It is the purest and most beautiful energy you can imagine and experience, the energy that fills you up. Fun is simply contagious. Can you imagine what all this has done to me? Being creative in the agency and working hard in the restaurant. Running, smiling, keeping everything going - and having fun? That was definitely missing. In the Network, on the other hand, I felt it, it was literally tangible. And that's why I made a firm resolution: If I really do start something new again, if I really do take off here in network marketing, then only by having fun. It should be my daily companion from now on! And I didn't just make this commitment to myself, I declared it to my entire team. All those who were there at the time, especially at the start of my new career. Fun, joy, lightness - these three terms were to carry, shape and define my actions in the future. That was to become my new, wonderful source of energy, because that is also a piece of "pp" - pure pink!

My 3rd starter bonus advice for you:
LET FUN INSPIRE YOU

Do everything you do with joy! You will not find a better driving force, better motivation and a better source for happiness and creativity in life! Whatever you do, do it with pleasure and joy. Allow yourself to laugh in everything you do. Let the joy of others infect you and in turn carry your cheerfulness to others in the same way. Then everything you do and make will be even more beautiful and easy! Network marketing? I'm in! So much, and so convinced, that I even wondered, slightly annoyed at myself, why I hadn't decided to start in this industry sooner. Even more, I thought angrily about why this opportunity had been kept from me until now and why no one had presented this business idea with enthusiasm earlier. Darn, how much time I had already wasted! How much I had already invested in other activities, but unfortunately without any really rewarding return and above all without any fun! What had I already missed in terms of happiness and pleasure. In this respect, I also recognized a certain professional secret: If fun and enjoyment are contagious and lead to such results, then what is going to happen when you share all of your happiness?

My 4th starter bonus advice for you:
SHARE YOUR LUCK!

If you give, you will receive! And those who share their own happiness by telling other people about their joy, and thus offering opportunities, multiply their happiness infinitely! That's what network marketing is all about. Spread your arms out: Because in this business you are not alone, it's about bringing as many great people into your circle as possible, in order to become successful together. But you can only do that if you are open to others and tell them about your business, about the quality and effectiveness, about the goodness of your products and genuinely from the bottom of your heart. That's exactly how I did it. My luck was that I experienced with my own body how the concept helped me. At a time when I was literally running on low batteries both mentally and physically. At the time, I had reached my limits due to overworking, in fact, I was past it. Pure sense of duty, ambition and unbridled self-confidence brought me there. Always with the false belief: "I can do it! I alone am strong enough and can endure it. If not me, then who can?" Today I know better: I put myself through far too much, and for whatever reason, I didn't pull the ripcord in time and it was long overdue. But thanks to the recommendation of my upline, my eyes were opened - in two ways. I felt the effect of the concept and what it did to me, my body, and my own vitality. On the other hand, I had the corresponding external effect and naturally spoke about it. I helped others, was able to improve their situation through my recommendation and actually did nothing else than what my upline had also done: She recommended something to my mother and I. Yes, she had spread her arms and brought us into her circle. She had shared her happiness with us and that's exactly what I was doing now. This is nothing other than network marketing at its purest! Experience, be convinced, recommend, and thus share your own happiness with others who then experience the same cycle and actively keep it going. And again, I ask you at this point: Is this really considered work? Or is it more like pleasure, inner satisfaction, and true fulfillment? Of course, there are always people who don't believe you, who don't follow the advice, the recommendation. So, what? Is that a reason to stop telling others about your impressions and positive experiences? Absolutely not. So why should it depress you if someone says no to your offer, to your advice? There is no reason for that. If you share your happiness with others, then there is no obligation for the other party to accept this gift. Everyone has their own free will. It is more important to tell as many people as possible about your happiness, about your joy. The more often you do this, the greater the number of those who will accept your offer. This is also called the "law of large numbers" - a mathematical term from the field of probability theory. I think for the positive effect of shared happiness there is a wonderful quote from Yoko Ono, who once said, "A dream you dream alone is only a dream. A dream you dream together is reality." There's something to that.

My 5th starter bonus advice for you:
TEAMWORK MAKES THE DREAM WORK!

Shared joy is double the joy! Along the lines of: Do good and talk about it because only then will more and more people follow you and join your vision!

In network marketing, you start with a dream or even a vision. It is the individual big goal that needs to be clearly defined and that's what I did back then. My primary goal was to have more time for myself, to escape the hamster wheel I was trapped in and by sharing my said happiness, more and more people joined. They joined my circle and passed on my recommendation once it had been given to them. As a result, we grew as a team and became stronger as a community.

Proportionally, the fulfillment of my dream also grew. I could never have done it so quickly, so powerfully, and so effectively alone. As a team with teamwork however, my dream became a reality. You can truly feel the power of a team. Just that incredibly beautiful, strong, deep feeling that flows through you when you rejoice in the community. It's nothing compared to what you feel when you experience happiness alone. I therefore quickly realized: Never alone, always in a team.

And I could only put this credo into practice and live it if I shared my experience with other people. I couldn't help it, it was an inner drive that made me do it. It was a conviction so strong that I could not and would not keep it to myself. For me, it would have almost been an offense to keep this unique opportunity that business network marketing holds all to myself. I had to. It was a matter of fairness, perhaps even decency, and humanity towards others.

6th Key: **PLAN**

City maps have almost disappeared from our world today. They are probably still known amongst a few and the older ones among us may even still have them. Somewhere with old travel documents or in the far corner of a shelf. Maybe a foldable road map is still hidden in the car door, who knows. In any case, they are relics from a seemingly different time. Compared to today, they were quite cumbersome to use, even though one was glad to have such a map in case of an emergency. The difficulty in using them was the often-complicated folding technique. Once "unfolded", it was always a most difficult task to re-fold the map according to the existing folds. But apart from that, you had to find your way around the map itself and this required at least a hint of geographical knowledge. If you had the map of a country as large as Germany in front of you and were looking for the hubs such as Hamburg while sitting in the south on the shores of beautiful Lake Constance, instead of on the Elbe in the north, you needed patience to finally slide your finger up and come across the Hanseatic city. It was no different when one looked for a street on a city map. Perhaps a map square was indicated, within which the eyes looked wildly back and forth. Always on the intense search for the right address. But how could one find the destination quickly and accurately? In contrast, nowadays it's comparably easy with a navigation system, which is usually pre-installed on your smartphone. Enter the exact address, click on search, and bam - you've reached your destination because you have a plan. You know the address, you know what to do, how to get there and the precisely defined destination is displayed in detail. Good! Practical! Useful! Time effective! And above all, safe - because the outlined way is always the most direct. If there are other routes or even detours, they are shown as separate alternatives. Hence, you can always be sure to find and use the fastest, the most direct route to your destination. It's funny however, that so many people handle things quite differently when it comes to their own lives, where many have no plan at all! They usually do not even have a goal in mind and instead wander through the uncertainties of everyday life. Often without knowing where the path will lead them. As an apparent excuse, people like to talk about a sense of adventure. To be honest, I would rather call it disorientation. Because if you run off without knowing where you're going, you're simply aimless, without a plan, and thus a little bit lost and such a person cannot arrive because the person does not know where the final destination is. How lost must such a person actually feel. It feels like running through the desert, where everything, absolutely everything looks the same. Nothing but sand, a few hills and a blue sky from which the sun bears down on you mercilessly. No matter where you look, everything looks the same or at least similar and to top it off, you're supposed to heed the call to start walking. Great, where to? In which direction? How do you get your bearings? How do you keep track of everything? And where do you want to go? Where do you want to arrive?

People without a plan in life wander around just as described in this example. Most of the time, they find themselves in a daily routine that offers them a minimum of regularity. Day in, day out, the same routine. A frustrating hamster wheel of boredom. Get up, have breakfast, drive to work, wait for the end of the day, drive back home, have dinner, watch TV, go to bed... and the next day looks exactly the same. Such people usually also know what their entire life will look like in thirty or forty years. Caught in a rut and monotony - school, a short fling, marriage, children, a vacation, a rented apartment or a townhouse, "surviving" every day as described above, waiting for retirement, then a little more TV and then that's it - the coffin is closed, this chapter of life is over. How tragic, how boring, and sad. Once again, there they are - those same gray pigeons that don't sing, warble, or chirp. Instead, they produce a dull, even irritating cooing. They are a far cry from the noble grace, magnificent appearance, and proud aura of a flamingo in its striking pink hue. These are two entirely distinct worlds.

But you can choose. Do you choose the meager security? Do you choose the completely finished path, which is dusty and dry and which you can trot along without having a plan of your own? Or do you have your own goals, goals that are close to your heart? Ones that make you enthusiastic, develop your zeal, motivate you, and which you absolutely want to achieve with enthusiasm, dedication, and fun? Do you want to go on the Formula One circuit of life? Are you ready to go above and beyond? Take off with enthusiasm and take off in a big way? You have the choice - and network marketing can be the number one highway to happiness and success for you. But - you need a plan. You need to know what you want and most importantly, you need to think about how you want to get there. What route are you willing to take? Are there obstacles holding you back? Are there insurmountable challenges for you or do they make you stronger than you already are? Do you accept challenges, or do you prefer to take detours? And most importantly - are you willing to pay the price? That is: Effort, exertion, work, sometimes sacrifice, diligence, and perseverance. This is the toll you have to pay to enter the expressway of life that leads to your personal happiness.

First of all, having a plan means working out a plan. You know your current location. You are where you are because you have decided to be there. It is the sum of your decisions that has led you to take one exit or another and has now brought you here. Now you mark your clear destination. Precisely defined. What do you want it to be? What does it look like? By when do you want to have reached it? Why is this goal so important to you? Can you describe it? Does the mere thought of it make your heart leap? Does this goal trigger longings and desires? Great - then it is also your very own individual destination. But now you also know what the route between your current location and your destination looks like. Now it's time to work out a plan that will make the distance yet to be covered become pinker and pinker the closer you get to your destination. Which way do you go? What intermediate goals do you set for yourself? What challenges can you expect? Are you adequately prepared for them? How much time do you give yourself to reach and master each of the individual stages? What do you have to do and complete for each stage? How and when do you want to arrive? And - very important - what happens when you have arrived? What is the next level? Do you have a goal behind the original goal? These are questions that, along with their answers, form your very own plan. It's your life plan, and it's great to have one because then you know what to do and don't wander around aimlessly. Now you have a plan. One that bathes you and your life in a wonderfully deep, brightly shining, striking pink. This plan is your 6th key to the Pink:Code and the four characteristics that follow will answer your question of how in depth.

THE FOUR MOST IMPORTANT FEATURES, THAT MAKE UP THE KEY: **PLAN**

1. HAVING A VISION - DEFINING & KNOWING WHY

The former Chancellor of Germany, Helmut Schmidt, once said in his all too familiar, slightly smug way: "Anyone who has visions should see a doctor...!" Okay, if we are talking about socio-political utopias, he was certainly right. In our case, it's rather the other way around. Those who have no vision for their lives are in danger of becoming mentally stunted because there cannot be a beginning, if there is no end goal! And somehow in all of us there is a deep longing for something. But what? If you ask people about their innermost hopes and dreams, then the two items "world peace" and "health" are always at the top of the list. The happy and contented life in a world of global harmony, in which everyone is doing splendidly, everyone is rich and only the weapons industry is forced to file for bankruptcy because no one needs these deadly goods anymore. Almost too good to be true. Do you also share these hopes and dreams? That would be very understandable.

After all, according to YouGov's 2020 survey, these were the most frequently expressed dreams according to a survey in seventeen countries around the world. However, these top dreams come with a tiny catch: they are virtually impossible to influence. Of course, you can start on a small scale by getting along well with your family, neighbors or other acquaintances and being considerate of one another. But you will hardly be able to influence world peace. What specific actions do you plan to take when one of the tyrants in this world goes crazy and mobilizes their army? Nothing! Except indignation, rage and grief there is not much left for the individual. In the matter of health, it also looks quite similar. Sure, you can eat healthier, work out more, and pay more attention to your personal well-being. But still: Nobody has ever died healthy. Sounds mundane, but it is the truth and there is nothing you can do about it. You also have to accept things as given. That is probably why the famous Serenity Prayer by the U.S. theologian Reinhold Niebuhr says: "Lord, grant me the serenity to accept things I cannot change…" Instead, dive into your inner self and search for your very personal longing. Something that would be a truly ideal state for you individually. What do you dream of in relation to yourself? What is close to your heart? What do you strive for and what would make you truly happy in life - or possibly even happier than you already are? Hard, isn't it? It's no wonder that according to surveys in Germany, eight out of ten people don't have an answer to the question of what their most important and biggest dream in life is. But isn't that a little frightening? After all, these supposedly desireless people are by no means blissfully happy. By no means at all. They are seekers. They just never questioned their visions, never searched for them and therefore live rather trivially through each day.

If you have found your personal answers to the question about your hopes and dreams, then you still have a long way to go until finally achieving them. Because your answer will only cover one topic, a broader area. For example, if you wish to be free, you must first define what freedom means to you. And to be free from what? The wish for one's own dream home is also often expressed. This example really shows perfectly what it means to concretize a hope or a dream. What is your dream home? Angled bungalow or gable roof construction? Ground level or with several floors? With or without an open kitchen? White exterior walls, standard, or clinker bricks? Large, park-like garden or small and cozy? With or without a pool? Carpet, wood, or tiled floor? Solar panels on the roof or wind turbines in the backyard? So many questions. But you see: The dream home is not the same for everyone, it must be outlined precisely and described in the finest of details and this applies to all dreams and visions. Because only if you know exactly what this individual dream looks like, will you also know what needs to be done to fulfill it.

Now you have been able to answer the question of the "how" – specifically the how of your dream. For a real vision though, there is another important aspect and that is the question of the "why." It is your why! The why of your life. It is the reason for your activity, from which your motivation, your personal driving force is fed. Why do you have this vision? Why do you want this dream of yours to come true? Why are you willing to do everything that is necessary for this desire? Why do you go "all in" for this goal and give everything you have? This "why" is your engine and therefore the "how" cannot be without the "why." Because you will inevitably ask yourself again and again throughout the stages towards your intermediate goals and the ultimate, final destination: Why am I doing all this? Why am I taking on this burden and why am I facing all these challenges? Is it worth it for me to reach my goal or is it enough to stop halfway, to be satisfied with what I have or have already achieved? This will make you stop and think. It will allow you to discover the real reason why you wanted to reach your personal big goal and why you started your journey towards success. This "why" will light your way and guide you. This "why" will tell you, why half the goal is not enough. Why half the distance isn't enough and why you have to muster up the necessary power to go further and take those last important steps! Do you feel the importance of your why? It is the answer to why you get up in the morning? Your why is your individual engine, your driving force, your thrust, your true pink!

2. FOCUS & GOAL ORIENTATION

If you capture the sun's rays with a magnifying glass and hold it in such a way that the rays are focused on a very central point, you cause the surface on which the sun's rays are centered to burn. It is similar with your focus. You must always keep your goal clearly in sight in order to ignite your inner fire. Okay, I'll say it once at this point, "Because that's the only way you can ignite the fire in others...!" I know, it is a catchy phrase in the network marketing business, a true oldie - but also a goodie! Because the essence of this sentence does not become diminished or less important just because the saying is well-known and mentioned often. On the contrary, precisely because it is so apt, it is also repeated again and again. But that is not the only thing that causes the sole focus and thus concentration on the goal, for only those who really focus on reaching the end point of their dream will also go straight for it. That means: Don't let yourself be distracted. Only one thing has priority: Your goal! That is exactly why it is called a "priority." You subordinate everything to your goal and the achievement of it because it has priority over everything else. Otherwise, your alleged "priority" would probably be treated as something subordinate and that's exactly what you don't want. Whoever is pink, is at the same time focused because this color catches everyone's attention. It is an active magnet and therefore leads your thoughts, your deeds, and your activities to one point, to one core - namely to your desired result. Do you notice how important your focus is? It is safe to say that focusing on something is one of the most important tools in your pink toolbox. That's why you focus on one thing, your goal, and not on several things in parallel. That would be like trying to hammer two nails into two completely different walls at the same time. That is also not possible. As such, it is impossible for us to focus on two or even more things. It's going in one direction and not two at the same time. Or have you ever seen someone who can go forward and backward at the same time? That's right, you can't. You don't even need to try that either. Your only and your exclusive direction should be towards the fire that burns within you and this should therefore be where you direct your focus.

And now you ask quite rightly - how! How do you do it? To answer this, I will once again use an everyday example. I bet you know the situation: You are sitting at your desk and want to get something done. You are still focused on your task, but then it happens: A totally unimportant e-mail arrives, which you quickly answer. A WhatsApp message follows, which you respond to in passing. Then the phone rings on your desk, followed by the parcel delivery man at the door, and shortly after that the neighbor whose parcel you've accepted. By the time you're back at your desk, five more e-mails have arrived, which you of course just want to answer quickly. Do you notice anything? Do you know this situation? Suddenly the entire morning is over, and you haven't made a single small step towards completing your actual task. On the contrary. What happens? You are most likely frustrated, irritated, and stressed because you let yourself be distracted and you haven't gotten any closer to your actual goal. How "un-pink" is that?

If you take a step back and look at this situation, one that we are all familiar with, it's like this: Life is not one big task, but a collection of countless challenges that you have to master every day. And the most difficult of all is not to lose sight of the overview and the actual goal. The question is: How do you achieve this goal as quickly and effectively as possible? And the answer is: Focus on success. To focus means: To concentrate on the essentials and use all your available energy to achieve a single, consciously chosen goal.

It's all about controlling your attention and never losing sight of what you're up to. Instead of letting yourself be distracted by e-mails, WhatsApp messages or supposed parcel delivery people, it's best to shut down your e-mail program right from the start, switch your cell phone to silent and uninstall the doorbell. When you sit down at your desk, you'll find peace not only on the outside, but also on the inside. This creates the best conditions for getting on with the day's work in a concentrated and speedy manner. These seemingly small measures, can also be applied to the somewhat larger interferences and threatening distractions. Resist the beginnings of possible disruptive factors or prophylactically exclude them from the outset. This is the best and most effective self-protection method. Focus can also be trained, and quite simply: Read a book while listening to a podcast for example. A podcast whose content would actually interest you, but concentrate only on the book! At first, it will certainly be difficult for you to grasp and mentally process the text you are reading in the book. You will probably even have to read some sentences or even paragraphs several times to completely understand and grasp the content, but the more often and intensively you train your focus and concentration, the easier it will be for you to mentally switch off the podcast and concentrate purely on the book. Just give it a try! You'll become mentally stronger and achieve your goals faster and seemingly easier. Ultimately, every process boils down to one simple key question that you need to keep asking yourself: Is what I'm doing right now really bringing me successfully closer to my actual goal? The more often you answer "yes" to this question, the more focused and goal-oriented you will be. But as soon as you answer "no" to your question even only once, you know that you have just taken a wrong turn and are on a detour or wrong path. Then there is only one thing for you to do: Get back on the right path! Focusing on a goal not only increases your chances of achieving it, but also your mood and motivation. So not only do you work faster, better, and more efficiently, you also work with far more enthusiasm. In other words, with a full glow of pink!

3. STRUCTURED - BEING ACTIVE WITH A SYSTEM

A true genius masters the chaos! As amusing as this sentence sounds on the surface, it is also often used as an excuse to specifically describe one's own chaos, the mess, the untidiness, and the lack of structure in one's approach. What good is the best plan if there is no structure to it? Even though our parents were always happy to lecture us on the importance of keeping things tidy and in order, they were right. If you're looking for something and can't find it right away because of untidiness and disorder, you're simply wasting valuable time and the nervous system is also unnecessarily strained. Tasks, challenges and pending work must be approached with a clear purpose, but also with system and structure. Anything else will not really get you anywhere.

But what is structured work? Does it mean to create a system or to proceed strictly according to a plan? First and foremost, it means mastering the art of prioritizing. A structured workday helps you to prioritize the many unfinished tasks and to work through them accordingly. In this way, you stay more focused on the task at hand and avoid stress that may arise. If you work in a structured way, you approach tasks with the help of an imaginary system and work through everything according to this. This order, which is rather individual, ensures that you work systematically through the upcoming activities. But why individually? Not everyone prefers the same parameters for quick, easy implementation. One person wants to do the things that need to be done quickly first, while another may prefer to have some conversations or do some brainstorming first before kicking things off.

Everyone has a different prioritization system, which is also somewhat based on how you feel you can best cope with and manage the order of the tasks. But one thing is certain - also because it has been scientifically proven several times: You should always start with the "biggest chunks." In other words, you should always do the most time-consuming work first, or the work that you would prefer to avoid first. This has a purely psychological background: Once the seemingly most difficult, unpleasant or time-consuming work has been done, everything that follows seems easy. Motivation increases, and you feel a large step closer to the goal - regardless of the number of outstanding tasks. On the other hand, if you keep putting off the unpleasant work, you put yourself under enormous pressure. It's like the famous sword of Damocles that then seems to dangle over you permanently. Even if you work off the other, supposedly easier tasks bit by bit, perhaps even quickly, you still have this one big challenge ahead of you. And it is precisely this that weighs you down, inhibits you, and makes the entire job seem more unpleasant overall. So, the rule applies: Get the hard part out of the way first!

With the following advice, you'll learn to work in an even more structured way:

1. Organize your desk
Do you tend to have a mess around you or does everything have its place? For a structured way of working, you also need a tidy desk. This does not have anything to do with being obsessed with order. If you don't, the restlessness in your environment will negatively influence you.

2. Avoid distractions
As with focusing, it is important to avoid distractions from internal and external sources. Accordingly, you ideally prepare yourself for the time when you are actively working on something upfront. How? Put simply: Distractions are taboo during this phase! And above all, your smartphone - unless it is a necessary tool for the tasks at hand - remains switched off. You should schedule a separate time slot outside of your concentrated working hours to deal with your communication, i.e. e-mails, WhatsApp or social media channels.

3. Set priorities
Of course, you have a lot to do. You have grand and ambitious goals and for their achievement you have to complete many tasks. But to find out what has priority and should be tackled first, you should prioritize using a certain system. It is recommended to follow the so-called Eisenhower principle, which helps you to manage your time even better.

This principle works by means of four categories:

- Important and urgent.
- Important, but not urgent.
- Not important, but urgent.
- Not important and not urgent.

These four answer-options result in four types of tasks, which determine the order in which you should complete them. Important and urgent tasks are best done first. You can tackle non-important and non-urgent tasks at the end.

4. Be mindful of your peak-times
Have you ever paid attention to when you are more motivated and focused during the day? You'll notice that you're much more active at certain times and your performance curve tends to drop at other times. Tasks that you have assigned a high priority should therefore be done at a time when your concentration is particularly high. During this time, you'll work more efficiently and achieve even better results.

5. Create routines for yourself
Routines give structure to your daily schedule. No, this has nothing to do with boredom. On the contrary because routines and this aforementioned daily plan help ensure that you work in a structured way.

6. Take breaksn
If you are constantly working in a structured and concentrated manner, you need regular breaks. Fresh air and exercise help you to clear your head again. This gives you more energy, which you can use to complete new tasks because creative phases also need the right counterpart - i.e.

rest phases. That means (re)sorting your thoughts, recharging your batteries, and becoming fully productive again.

4. "DOUBLE CC" – CONSISTENCY WITH CONTINUITY

Once pink, always pink! No, unfortunately not because in order to become and stay pink, you need to do something else, and that's keeping it up with consistency and continuity. Sounds rather simple, and it basically is, but nevertheless some people stumble here and there.

Having a plan for yourself and your dreams is one thing but you also have to apply it and follow it accordingly. Plans that you have for the sake of having them on the other hand, are of no use at all. It's as if you have a key to the gate of happiness, but you never put it in the lock to open it.

But now you already have the 6th key to the Pink:Code in your hand - so use it consistently, everywhere, and continuously until the lock finally opens. What I'm trying to tell you is that you shouldn't just dust off your perfect plan every now and then and activate it on a whim. It deserves it and so do you - that your plan for individual happiness is always spread out before you, and that you continuously put it into action throughout your life. Most importantly, as already mentioned before, with everything you have. Because it works particularly well when you give your best. Remember, you have to be all in!

Having a workable plan in life and vision is not serendipity, but rather personal bliss. Why? Because pretty much everyone longs for it - sometimes more and sometimes less obviously. But only very few have such a plan. Well, now you can see what a "lucky pink mushroom" you are! Not because few people have a vision or their own desires, but rather because most people lack the opportunity make their dreams come true. The dream alone is of no use if it remains a dream. The point is to make it a reality. Go ahead and be a little like little Pippi Long-stocking, whose motto was: "I'll make the world the way I like it!" That's right, but what Pippi can do, you can do too. You've got what it takes and even more: The necessary tool, namely your business, network marketing! Where else do you have the freedom and the opportunity to make your visions come true? Only this great industry offers you that.

It is therefore pivotal to stick to the plan with consistency and continuity. Let me explain why and how consistency and continuity go hand in hand. You get up - and the first thing you do is plan your day! Remember, together we are working on the 6th key to the great Pink:Code - the plan. And to every plan belongs another plan. The plan for the plan! If you have a plan for your day, then you know what needs to be done and what tasks lie ahead of you. Now the already mentioned priority list comes into play. What do you start with? What comes at the end? The four items from the list in the previous paragraph will help you. Now the consistency comes into play because the very first thing you're going to do is make a commitment. Something that you will now write in bold capital letters on your priority list every day. CONSISTENCY!

But how does this work? Of course, this list must also be worked through consistently. Without ifs and buts! That means: No exceptions, no distractions. Especially the already mentioned distractors have to be switched off. Consistency also includes the appropriate language you use. Stop using phrases like: "I should, would have, could...!" Instead, become completely pink from now on and switch to the fully active phrases of: "I want to, I can, I will...!" Because otherwise you always leave a back door open, from which you could secretly and quietly escape from your responsibilities to yourself. Best not to though, because to be consistent also means to be firm with yourself and the inner voice of comfort. It's about remaining true to yourself and demonstrating the appropriate assertiveness, even if it sometimes feels uncomfortable for you. Being consistent with yourself means a certain form of self-management. It means that you implement things completely according to the plan.

And you can teach yourself this "consistent self-management" if you are not yet as consistent as you would like to be. First of all, your daily goals on the priority list must be realistic in terms of implementation. If you set out to do something in the morning that realistically takes at least a whole day, you will fail. Why then lie to yourself? The only thing you will get out of this is frustration. Completely unnecessary! And what happens then? You start to agonize, because you think it won't work anyway. Look at your priorities, what is feasible and compare this with your competences. If you have never had twenty appointments in one day for example, but only one or two, then you won't be able to change everything in one fell swoop. Ambition? Yes! Ambitious goals? Absolutely! But they must be achievable and remain so.

The already mentioned routines and systems help with consistency and thus generate double the value. An almost ideal trick is to reward yourself - but also punish yourself. No joke. Treat yourself to something that's not an everyday occurrence once you've worked through your day perfectly according to your plan and priority list. Whether it's a special treat, a small gift for yourself - it doesn't matter. But if, contrary to expectations, you have not implemented your day 1:1 as intended, then it is time to reprimand yourself. Be it that you are active for half an hour longer than planned as a "consequence" or that you do some unfinished work at home.

As you can see, being or becoming pink is not a no-brainer. Those who manage it however, know what they get out of it: Such a person shimmers only in the most beautiful and dazzling shades! And the plan contributes a significant part to your pink intensity.

ONLY THOSE WHO CAN LEAD THEMSELVES CAN LEAD OTHERS.

REMEMBER WHERE YOU CAME FROM, EVEN AS YOU GROW AND DEVELOP. STAY *Humble*

Leading with heart means, becoming more and more pink

In German there is a well-known phrase that can be literally translated to "the tone makes the music." It implies that it is not only about what you say but how you say it. Paying attention to the tone and delivery is extremely important in order to convey the intended meaning and intent. Therefore, everything I do, I do with heart and soul. The emphasis, however, is on the syllable "heart." Have and show your true heart. This is something that humanity needs today more than ever. This is exactly the kind of sprit I have experienced permanently in the team - first and foremost from my upline and the absolute top executives.

But what is behind it? Let me tell you. It's not a leadership style, it's more a culture, a fundamental mindset because it goes far beyond how to lead properly. Anyone in an employment relationship today will have experienced this often enough. That is, instead of recognition, superiors often say: "Not complaining is praise enough"…Wrong! Every human being is looking for recognition and positive confirmation - in private as well as in business! Unfortunately, the reality often looks different. What good it is to be aware of this and to handle it differently. I have previously mentioned the power of positive thinking and just as equally a positive way of dealing with one another is just as much a part of it. We don't have to make life more difficult than it already is, right? A kind word here, a smile there, a friendly gesture - all this makes life worth living and pleasant. Who would lose anything by praising someone else for a job well done? Praise and recognition are as important as they are fundamental features in network marketing. How nice! This is exactly what I've experienced from the beginning, and I would like to pass it on to you because it has always done me good. I feel comfortable in such an atmosphere. You can let yourself go, open up, and positive energy flows through you and sustains you. To put a smile on someone's face with praise and recognition is a wonderful experience. Give it a try if you haven't already. You will be amazed by the power this kind of positive interaction awakens and the good things you get in return.

"Leading with the heart" does not mean overlooking everything else. I can point out a grievance, a mistake, or a difficulty to someone without letting the undertone of accusation resonate. If I am told how I can do something better, I do not have to get the feeling that I have failed. Rather, everyone benefits if I then draw lessons from it that help me to move forward. Because in the future I will do something better than before with a positive feeling - and that for the benefit of everyone. "Leading with the heart" has already paid off in full. This positive culture of togetherness instead of the "from the top down" has a tremendous impact. Because this spirit spreads and is noticeable in all practical applications - through the fun and the emerging joy in all business activities and private sphere as well. It is appreciation across the board. I love it and I stand up for the fact that my life in all its facets participates and is determined by it.

This interaction and culture of togetherness, sustained me, especially in the early days of my then new business. This especially encouraged me to move forward with enthusiasm and to an extent which allowed me to climb up the career ladder continuously. Celebrations, awards for achievements, making new discoveries, and inspiring each other - to experience something like that in a team within a large community is really something unique and remains unforgettable for me - especially as far as my beginnings in the business are concerned. Fear of making mistakes? I've never been afraid of making mistakes, and I'm even less afraid of them now because of this appreciative way of dealing with people. Because everyone makes mistakes. They are largely responsible for giving us the chance to learn substantially from our actions and experiences.

If you ask me today why I am successful in network marketing, I will gladly list the starter bonus advice I have mentioned so far. To this day, they are the pillars of my business that I rely on and in addition, there are some insights that you learn over time and whose significance becomes clearer and more apparent each time. That's the kind of thing you memorize. These are fundamental insights that I then pass on to each of my team partners. They help you make it, just like I made it. A statement to which I always add an explanation because it is so important: What I have achieved so far in the network marketing industry makes me very happy and I have every right to feel a bit proud about it. And yet it's not really anything special.

Why do I say this? Because anyone can make it, just as millions of other people before me, have also made it. That in no way diminishes my past performance or my track record. Not at all. I just want to make it clear that it is far less remarkable than it seems at first glance because that's exactly the kind of success anyone can achieve in this business. Anyone! You as well as me! Always under one condition: You have to want to do your best every day! You have to be diligent!

If you don't want to be, you won't get far in this business. That's part of being honest. You can't win a pot of gold in network marketing with laziness and comfort. For us, it's all about getting out of your comfort zone and not getting into the comfort zone. Once success and triumphs have been achieved, the world looks different again. On the way there, work is waiting for you. A lot of work, but also work that is fun and extremely enjoyable.

I always say: Success begins at home! I am very aware of that! Especially in the field of referral marketing. Therefore, always do your best where you are. In your environment. That is your starting point and do your best with what you have! Because your environment cannot be changed to your liking. At home means: With you! With you and where you move. This is where you know your way around, where you are in your center, in your core. There you know the ways, know the channels and know where to look and listen. There your word counts for something. There your advice carries weight. There you can act and know how to react. Even though the network industry gives you the opportunity to build up and run your business from anywhere, it is important, especially at the beginning, to start at your own center.

Move out into the big wide world later? Other cities, other countries, other continents? Sure, why not? But before that, you should start with yourself and your own sphere of influence. From your center, you can then draw ever wider circles. Because: Success begins with you - also where you are! For me, this inversion means that you also have to let go. To move forward without turning around. To be curious and open-minded towards the new, instead of looking back wistfully. So why start something new in the first place? Because whatever you left behind you didn't satisfy you, or not completely. I loved my studies. I also loved the agency work, where I could really let off steam creatively. Working in a restaurant also taught me a lot and I gained a lot of experience. But I wasn't happy, I wasn't satisfied, it wasn't perfect and certainly not how I imagined my life would be in the long run. So, I had to let go because the new attracted me and offered me sensational prospects. With this attitude, I realized that I already had the wings - I just had to fly off. But when and where to? I could no longer change anything about my past anyway. That piece of life had already been lived. But now I was ready for a new great journey. That was what was on my mind and motivated me as well. Honestly? Doesn't that excite you too? Don't you sometimes think what else could there be? Just fly, spread your wings and soar to your dream. You will realize that you can change yourself as well as the whole world a little bit. Ask yourself these questions every day: Can you fly? Do you want to fly? Do you want to change your life? Do you even want to change the world? Then set out on the journey as I set out to do. Spread your wings, take a run-up and just take off ...

SUCCESS STARTS AT HOME

IT STARTS WITH YOU — WHAT ARE YOU WAITING FOR?

7th Key: **PARTNERSHIP**

What one can hardly accomplish, two can accomplish more easily! Sounds logical and it is! Yet it is sometimes not so easy to convince some die-hard lone wolves or soloists of the many benefits of a partnership. In fact, this conviction often only occurs when the benefits of a partnership are experienced first-hand and in daily interaction. You probably now think of terms like freedom, speed, self-sufficient action and that you don't have to justify yourself to others, are not dependent on anyone else and can absolutely decide for yourself. Yes, this may all seem true, but nevertheless these apparent advantages do not stand up, especially when examined more closely and when you look beneath the surface of these weak arguments. One crucial reason why Network Marketing is so effective is that it is a team sport, not an individual competition! The system is designed for teams, not for solo performers. It works best when you build genuine partnerships that form a cohesive team focused on mutual support, collaboration, friendship, and powerful performance. Seemingly obvious, isn't it? Or can you imagine the world's best volleyball player, for example, standing by themselves on the court and playing alone against others? How would that work? Not only that, with all their extravagant skills, they wouldn't stand a chance against a complete team. Moreover, they would hardly be able to use and utilize their skills, or at least only to a lesser extent. And the attractiveness of the sport per se would suffer greatly from their solo ambitions. Passing? Tactics? Perfect sets for the next smash, top positional play - none of that would be possible and the outstanding competence and skill of this top player would play no role at all because they lack a complete team. One in which they are one of several great players and thus form an almost unbeatable team. In network marketing, it's identical. Here, too, you will only be able to use and live out all your skills, all your abilities and all your strengths if you work as part of a team and are on an equal footing with the others. That's what makes you powerful, that's pure power - and that's some of the purest and most radiant pink you can imagine. Now you're in the Pink:Code and to top it off, your team is intensely glowing inside and out in this wonderful, eye-catching, warm and bold color.

But what constitutes a genuine partnership? What are the benefits and how do you reach the stage of an intact, harmonious, and resilient partnership? What do you have to look out for when maintaining this special relationship? And most importantly, how do you find a partner in the network business in the first place? Because - once again - your very first partnership is just the beginning of your network existence. Such great prospects - but nevertheless a partnership is starting. Only from many such "direct duos" is a team formed, where everyone pulls together in one direction and works, thinks and strives! Thus, the most common mistake in a partnership is usually based on a wrong definition or misunderstanding of the partnership. If someone believes that a partnership means one partner does all the work, then the foundation and equal footing are missing. Saying "You do it because I already have done it" doesn't count in a partnership. An intact partnership is not about shifting the work from oneself to others and retreating back into one's own comfort zone. Lying around doing nothing while the other person works themselves into the ground? A no-go! That would make a mockery of the purpose, including all the advantages of a partnership. This also not only applies in business, but also in private relationships!

It is much rather about togetherness and the feeling of a closed community. What stands out? It is about the "together" in togetherness, the "common" and the "unity" in community! All this speaks
for itself! However there still more to it. Because a partnership is also like completing a puzzle, complementing each other. If one partner is lacking in a particular skill, the other partner can often make up for it with their own strengths. By combining their individual strengths, competencies, and positive qualities, they can create a more powerful team. In this way one effectively bundles together the existing strengths and doubles one's own impact, which is why in network marketing this is often referred to as the "power of duplication" because that's exactly what it is. With the formation of every new, intact partnership, one's own strengths and competencies are multiplied at the same time. This is not only sensible, but above all extremely effective and efficient. Partnership and teamwork ultimately mean moving "away from the I and towards the we" - mutuality instead of individuality, diversity instead of monotony, togetherness instead of isolation. Perhaps you can think of even more things that come from a good partnership. But what defines a good partnership in the first place? It is marked by openness and transparency because a two-way relationship like this always needs an extremely important and fundamental foundation on which it is created and exists: And that is trust. Only when both know that they can rely on each other completely, does a partnership work. This is the only thing that nourishes and strengthens it. An essential part is therefore communication. Talking to each other, exchanging ideas, always being on the same page, on a unified common ground for conversation

- this is an equally important and valuable building block that always keeps mutual trust at an extremely high level and permanently supplies it with fresh, positive energy.

In network marketing however, there is another special feature that constitutes a partnership. It is much more than just a "strategic tandem." In my business, it's about turning partnerships into friendships. Something that makes up the Pink character and always brings me a very special kind of joy in this wonderful business. How nice does it feel to climb to the summit of success together with friends, or to accomplish one's own hopes and dreams together, instead of being alone or only with your "colleagues." A "strategic partnership" is more purpose-driven. Partnership is a valuable compromise when it comes to achieving goals that would be difficult to achieve alone. Some people only enter into partnerships because they see a benefit in working together towards a common goal. However, this transactional approach is not the kind of partnership that is valued in network marketing and in the Pink:Code. Partners become friends for life. Together a dazzling flock of brightly shining pink flamingos is formed who achieve, enjoy, and celebrate their successes together - with positive pink power parties!

THE FOUR MOST IMPORTANT FEATURES, THAT DEFINE THE KEY: **PARTNERSHIP**

1. DOES IT FIT OR NOT?

You cannot put something together that does not belong together. This is not just a simple fact, it's a necessary condition for any kind of social cohesion or shared experience. Even more, it is a question of mutual respect. Anyone who works on a 10,000-piece jigsaw puzzle, adding piece after piece, can only do so because these pieces fit, without compromises having to be made. But if, in the end, the last piece should end up having a completely different shape and structure than the last free gap, then no one would even think of forcing and squeezing this piece of the puzzle into the free space, right? "If it doesn't fit make it fit!" A nice, well-intentioned saying and sometimes also extremely useful in application, but not applicable in this context. The last piece does not fit – end of story. Because even if a gap remains, the puzzle and the parts that have been put together so far all still hold together perfectly. Even if it were somehow inserted with its incorrect tabs, it would still always remain noticeable and out of place. It is not much different in a partnership, which later settles in and fits into a whole team. Only if the duo is made up of two parts that really fit well together, and also want to be together, does it have a real chance to become a functioning partnership.

This includes having a shared level of understanding. What does this mean exactly? In order to work together in a solution-oriented and purposeful manner, it requires not only an adequate level of knowledge but also mutual acceptance as a starting point. That means you have to take the other person as they are and decide for yourself that you like them exactly as they are. If you ask yourself now whether this does not collide with the previously explained personality development, then I can reassure you: No, it does not! Because a personality grows from the basis of what already exists. Certain things, virtues, attitudes, and character traits must be inherent from the outset. Similar to the growth of a rose plant, which develops gradually, first forming the stem, then the leaves, thorns, and finally the bud, from which a beautiful flower blooms. All of this is a process, a development.

It is no different with a partnership in the beginning. You decide whether you like the basic values that have already been created, from which the personality is then formed, sharpened and individualized more and more. With this existing "mental foundation" to compare and assess your own convictions, qualities, and perspectives. Now comes the decisive moment: Does it fit or not? And to say it upfront, this is not an easy decision, but one that has to be made with a high degree of respect and responsibility because it has far-reaching consequences - for you, for the other person and for your team. For you, because agreeing to a partnership means walking the path together in the future. You have taken on a certain amount of responsibility for this joint journey because you have agreed to contribute, to care, to share, to help and to be there for the other person. You will both benefit from each other in the future. And what is valid for you at this moment, is of course also valid in reverse for the other person. Of course, your agreement to the partnership also has consequences for the other person. The mere fact that you are now giving them access to the network marketing industry and at the same time offering them the chance to share and fulfill their visions and dreams with you, is making a significant contribution. So, if these are not consequences of a decision, what are? It's a similar story with your team, because saying yes to a partnership with someone impacts your colleagues as well. The atmosphere of the new-found togetherness is contagious and has an influence.

Does it further brighten the mood? Does it contribute to a positive team spirit? Does the new partnership also motivate others or does it have an inhibiting and disruptive effect? Does it in any way negatively affect the team, the mood? The answer to the question "does it fit or not" is therefore of great importance and has corresponding consequences.

Your honesty is therefore also of extreme importance. This is not about a "maybe" or a "let's see." A partnership is not a simple experiment, because people cannot be easily discarded like a toy that one loses interest in after a short while. It is important to make a clear, unambiguous decision: Yes or No! And the yes here does not mean "forever and ever", but it is the yes to start the partnership. It is the acceptance of a person and their qualities, of their current "I am who I am." It doesn't mean that one has to maintain this relationship if, based on the current situation, this partnership should develop into two different, no longer compatible directions. You can now see how significant the decision is and the responsibility that comes with it. It also makes clear that it takes courage and decency to say no. That means, if after careful consideration you conclude: It doesn't fit! This answer is also possible and is part of your arsenal for decision-making. You owe this to yourself, to your team, but above all to the other person. It is a matter of respect! And thus, a question of how pink you are and how pink you act!

2. RECIPROCITY ON EQUAL FOOTING

To be clear: There is no such thing as a unique partnership in network marketing, that can be strictly classified according to a scheme and special characteristics. You can't create a list on which you tick the boxes to determine whether a partnership will be successful. It is exactly the differences that ensure the necessary diversity. That is why a successful

Pink business partnership rests on several pillars at the same time, one of which is equality. This produces valuable intellectual balance and stands for acceptance, respect, and identical values. It means: Both are worth the same. Neither is above or below the other. There is a mutually accepted, wanted and welcome parity - despite all differences. Both partners respect each other and neither tries to dominate the other. This is however, only possible if both are prepared to restrain their individual egos accordingly and to keep them in check. Especially when two "alpha animals" meet. When two people who like to lead, who like to set the tone, and who feel particularly comfortable in the front row are confronted with each other.

You will probably ask yourself now, which requirements are necessary so that a correspondingly equal partnership in network marketing can arise in the first place. A complete balance is difficult to achieve without work and without concessions and mutual understanding. In other words: Both have to want to take steps towards each other! Mutual appreciation and the will to walk the path together makes it possible - and just as necessary! Because if only one partner moves while the other wants to stay in the same place, both will inevitably move further away from each other. For this reason alone, open, honest, and appreciative communication is absolutely essential. Where do you want to go? Where can I accompany you? Where do we stand? What is our common goal? These are all questions whose answers will make the common ground clear and thus manifest the meaning of a partnership. If both have the same intentions, both are moving in the same direction and towards the same goal, and both agree on the correspondingly same path, then one can confidently speak of equality. Both have virtually the same location, the same path, and the same goal in their community. They walk together and use their strengths accordingly on this path to meet challenges with twice the strength and overcome them. This is a perfect partnership on equal footing. Both partners are aware that they are tackling the same work, tasks, and obstacles together on their common path, despite all their differences in personal experience and background.

Respectful interaction, mutual trust and competence, responsible action and appreciation - all these aspects are thus fundamental prerequisites for a business partnership on equal footing. But there is one more important aspect: Communication. We have already touched on this here and there in the Pink:Code but in this context, it's not about communication itself, but about the way people communicate with each other.

After all, in order to exchange ideas on equal footing, both must be willing to do so in the first place. There must be a desire for constructive communication! Nobody has to say something to somebody else or to give orders to somebody. In this moment one would have left the common foundation of equal footing. Who wants to reach common goals together and contributes in equal parts to the success in their own way. That is the linchpin of the process. And this includes that not only one part constantly gives the direction - at worst still by the imperative - and the other follows obediently and willingly. Because if there are different views and interpretations of the way, they must be discussed openly, fairly, and honestly. Something completely normal. You cannot always agree. Different people have equally different views. However, through dialogue on equal footing, we then struggle to find the best possible solution and that solution has to be found. A solution that produces two winners and does not result in a compromise at the expense of the other. A partnership that lives by these rules is sure to last quite a long time, because it is complimentary, is constantly vibrant inside and always remains fresh and agile. Such a cooperation demonstrates that differences are the spice of life, but that everything ultimately ends in a joint resolution. One that is goal-oriented, useful, functional, and promising for both. That is Pink in the highest degree!

Communication in business partnership - four small, simple, pink pieces of advice, for even better mutual understanding:

1. Let your counterpart finish, do not interrupt and please do not try to prove them wrong immediately.

2. If you speak slowly, people listen to you! If you talk too fast, you always make a rushed and overwhelmed impression. If you want to find a solution, give yourself time to catch your breath while speaking.

3. Sometimes it is better not to answer quickly, but to think first. This reduces the often common "offensive tactics" and can create a better conversational climate.

4. Ask how your opinion is received. Are you being understood correctly? Or does your counterpart perceive your remarks merely as "complaining" rather than as a desire for improvement?

3. RECOGNIZING POTENTIAL

AEveryone talks about potential. So, do I, because it's an important building block in the Pink:Code. The term "potential" has been booming for some time now. It comes up again and again and is used in many different ways. There is the potential discovery, the potential activation or the potential development. Anyone who succeeds in fully developing his or her potential is on the road to success. Someone like that has made it. Sounds good, doesn't it? So, let's go for that potential. But what is actually behind this word?

Like everything in life, potential has several pillars and consists of different elements. Only when all of them interact successfully is the full potential available. On the one hand, there is talent, i.e. natural gifts which you were more or less born with. These can be cognitive talents such as intelligence, intuition, mathematical understanding, logical thinking or a good memory. They can also creative talents like artistic or musical talent, a certain feeling for learning languages, a great inventive talent, the art of recognizing problems and wanting to solve them. Last but not least, there are the coordinative talents such as manual dexterity, athleticism, creating structures, organization or the ability to coordinate.

Another pillar is knowledge and skills that a person has and that belong to the potential. These are acquired by people during their lives through active learning. It begins in school and continues in training, studies, further education, qualifications, but also in daily life, in play, sports and generally in leisure time. All of this is not to be confused with the respective competencies of a person. After all, they are the sum of talents, knowledge, and skills. The combination of these three components reveal, for example, action competence, technical and methodological competence, social competence, communicative competence, or personal competence.

Finally, there is personality. It is an important factor because a person's personality is the combination of various components that manifest in a very individual and specific way. Colloquially, this is also referred to as the "nature" or "temperament" of a person. For example, there are women and men who are more introverted or extroverted, more creative or analytical, more structured or chaotic, more conscientious or superficial, more outgoing or distant. There are people who prefer to work with others and those who prefer to work alone in a quiet room. All of this occurs along a spectrum. Personality is the spice that adds individuality to one's potential and makes them stand out from the crowd.

The discovery, activation and development of the potential is again a constant, permanent process. Every experience changes one's potential because even the smallest things contribute to expanding and modifying potential. As you see, there are many different elements for starting to discover potential. Only in the second step is it a matter of activating and unfolding dormant potential. All of this, by the way, does not happen at the push of a button. It is a process that progresses differently for each person and takes differing amounts of time. Two things are certain, however:

1. It is simply worth it.
2. People who ignore their potential live far below their means - and are usually dissatisfied with their lives sooner or later.
Their frustration stems from the fact that they are not utilizing their full

potential. People have an innate drive to use their full potential and feel unsatisfied when they are not given the opportunity to do so. But what exactly? That, in turn, is the crux. It's more like a feeling that bubbles up inside of them and tells them, "That can't be all! There must be more!" Definitely, but what? The constant under-utilization and self-doubt frustrates, demotivates, annoys, and stresses them. On the other hand, those who can actively use, develop, and live out their potential - their talents, knowledge, skills, and personality - find it easier to overcome challenges and experience life in a more intense, beautiful, and fulfilling way. Exactly this ease, is the foundation for success.

Do you notice something? Yep - that's precisely why it's worth discovering the potential in another person! This potential can be the sparkling source to your next pink, which will start to shine and glow even more. This person can be the source that pushes your network business even further. Yes, who will perhaps even shoot it upwards and make it explode like a bright pink firework. That's what makes the network marketing business so exciting because you never know beforehand whether the new team partner will be a shooting star, a progressive late bloomer, a perennial favorite, or someone who has a lot of talent and great potential, but who is still not the best fit for your business.

This realization should make one thing clear to you: Never judge and evaluate a person before you have really gotten to know them but invest everything you have to offer in them. Discover, explore, and unlock their hidden potential because that person could be the one who changes your entire life overnight. But until you try it, you won't be able to know. So, don't just give another person a chance, but first of all give yourself a chance! You will feel the pink potential and how much radiance it develops.

4. BE THE BEST VERSION OF YOURSELF

Have you ever wondered what the best version of yourself would look like? How you would live, how you would look and what you would create? Or what would be different about you? Would you even know what you want to change? Do you even want change or are you satisfied with what you see in the mirror? If not, then why not start right now? No one is stopping you. I'm an absolute fan of always working on yourself to become the best version of yourself - the theme of this chapter!

But to tackle that, there's one critical question at the very, very top of your to-do list: What would the best version of yourself even be like? My advice to you: Why don't you use the next three minutes, grab a piece of paper, a pen or even your smartphone or tablet and just get started by answering the following questions:

▷   What is the best version of myself?
▷   How am I living as the best version of myself?
▷   What do I look like as the best version of myself
▷   What would I be capable of as the best version of myself?

If you were able to answer these four questions, then everything should be clear and you now know what to do, don't you? Of course not. If it were that simple, then almost only "best versions" would be running around. That would actually be nice but the reality looks a bit different, isn't it? But why not take up this challenge anyway? That's exactly what it's all about: Recognizing and acting accordingly. By asking yourself and getting to know yourself, you now know what the best version of you could be like. What do you want to change? If you know why you have identified this and what the benefits are in changing, then you have at the same time discovered and identified your motivation. It is your "why" - why you want to change something about yourself and why it will benefit you. What logically follows next is to start actively doing something because after all, what would be the alternative to becoming your best version? Is there one at all? What would your life look like and how would it develop if you were to pause and not become active? The answer to this question will be motivation enough for you - I am sure of it. Do you want to be or become as you imagined when answering the four questions above?

Then all you have to do is ask yourself the famous question that keeps coming up in this book because it's crucial: How? I don't want to leave you alone with this question because I really want to open the way to the Pink:Code for you, using the individual keys. So, ask yourself: How do I make my ideal vision of myself become a reality? To find the appropriate answers, think about the following questions again and write down your answers - but take your time.

▷ What are the milestones that I need to achieve in order to live like the best version of myself?
▷ What changes do I need to make to my lifestyle to look and feel like the best version of myself?
▷ What skills are necessary to create what I want to become as the best version of myself?

Your answers to these questions will help you do what it takes! Important: Dare to listen to yourself. Trust yourself! Always remember: Nobody knows you as well and as long as you know yourself. In general, there are always ways to improve yourself. We are all subject to change and time teaches us a lot of lessons. You should definitely take advantage of these lessons. If you recognize mistakes and learn from them, you are guaranteed to become a better version of yourself. Almost automatically. And one more thing: Listen to your inner voice and thus to your own desires! These things don't come to you simply by chance, but rather from your innermost and deepest self!

SEVEN ACTIVITIES TO SUPPORT YOU ON YOUR JOURNEY TO BECOMING YOUR BEST SELF:

1. Get enough sleep
Nothing mitigates stress like sleep and it is the best source of energy to have enough strength for upcoming challenges! Seven to eight hours are optimal!

2. Get up early(er)
Successful people are early risers. The reason for that is because in the morning your power reserves and energy depots are one hundred percent recharged. Harness your power and be more productive while your brain is optimally supplied with blood.

3. Exercise in the morning
No need for any intense sport or workout, but a little movement will do the trick. Do a hundred steps in the morning like I do after you have written in your gratitude diary, or even ten minutes of stretching and push-ups will also help. You'll find it easier to focus on your other im-

portant goals and your brain will be supplied with more oxygen, which in turn will help you be able to solve the problems of the day more quickly. Remember: The early bird gets the worm.

4. Take cooler showers
It relieves stress, helps to clear your head, gets your circulation going and on top strengthens your immune system.

5. Dress well
What does this have to do with your best version? A lot! Because this version looks great, and is therefore well-groomed. Plus, a better outfit also promotes your mental health - because you feel better and act better accordingly. The old saying: "Clothes make the man" has its justification.

6. Focus on positive things
Easier said than done! But if you read books about success or the successes of others over breakfast, you'll be motivated and won't be in a bad mood. Give it a try! Or consciously choose positive literature or podcasts. Just leave the newspaper and the TV with bad news off.

7. Practice gratitude
In the morning, write down three things you are grateful for and in the evening, what you have achieved, what you have succeeded in, and what you are grateful for that day! You will be surprised how many great positive things you will suddenly write down!

I'm happy to see you are getting closer and closer to your ideal version, step by step. That's great! But do you know what's truly the very best part? Now that you know roughly how it works and how you managed to recognize what your best version is, you can actively share your knowledge. You can start helping others to become their best version in turn. Wouldn't that be a worthwhile goal, especially in a partnership that is mutual anyway? Sure, it would! And you now know how it works. You have the key in your hand - the precious, valuable seventh key to the Pink:Code.

BECOME A TALENTSCOUT IN YOUR TEAM.

ENCOURAGE YOURSELF AND OTHERS

TO BECOME THE BEST VERSIONS OF THEMSELVES.

YOU YOURSELF ARE THE GREATEST *Wonder*

S for Start – this is the only way to reach your goal

You know that a door always opens as soon as you close another one. That's nice to know and this moment is always exciting. Out of the dreariness and into the most exciting adventure there is - life! Your life! You have the potential to shape as you like because that's how you experience the greatest power, which drives you and seems to make the impossible possible. It is never too late for that. I can still hear my grandma today, telling me, "Stefanie, you must have made it by the time you're fifty!" A belief system that used to be deeply and firmly anchored in me. It's no wonder, considering how often I had to listen to this statement. Today I know however, that it's baloney! The only thing I have to manage is to shape my life according to my own wishes, to listen to myself and to consider my needs. I have to take care of my happiness. Whether that is at the age of fifty, or sooner or later - it doesn't matter. But I have to let go, fly away and take a chance! The main thing is to get started, no matter what. After all, no one can know in advance whether they will reach their personal goal.

IMPORTANT FOR YOU TO KNOW:

The path towards the goal begins the day you start to take one hundred percent responsibility for your actions! Without excuses, without ifs and buts! You go "all in" and "all in" means: everything without conditions.

However, if you give everything and put all your eggs in one basket, then that is by no means arrogant, risky or even irresponsible because there is always one factor that you can and need to be able to count on: That is YOU! You are the one you can best rely on. You know who you are. You know yourself! Who do you count on, if not yourself? You are always there for yourself, aren't you? Then you are also your best safety in your actions, life and deeds. I asked myself the question then: Am I ready for this next and new step? Am I ready to fly? Am I ready to give my best? Am I ready to take responsibility for myself? Am I ready to look forwards and no longer look backwards? Yes, I was - and I am! That's why I give everything, absolutely everything. All or nothing, that's the motto.

For me it was certain: All the way! I seized my chance fully. I decided, yes, I will! No compromises, no excuses! Because I trusted myself! I was ready. Are you too? There's only yes or no! But you will most certainly say yes, won't you? Yes, to you and yes to your life as you really want to lead it? If that's the case, and I hope it is with all my heart, then it's about sharing that happiness by giving others a new, intense, and great vision for their lives. For then you ask others: Are you ready too and if so, what do you bring to the table? What attributes make you stand out from the crowd as we go "all in" together and walk this path side by side? This is a question of trust because if I am willing to give my all, I can also experience what you bring to the table. Over the months since 2018, many people have been willing to spread their wings and soar towards their personal success. Our community grew and grew. I could also say at this point: We became pinker and pinker! With this, I believe I have already explained to some extent the question of "how" but I want to elaborate on it a bit more at this point.

My principle here is three-fold and I call it the "ASP" plan. To me, this system is practical, effective, sensible, safe and, above all, extremely pragmatic. If this simple and useful "Pink Success Plan" appeals to you and convinces you, then I can tell you: Congratulations - you will surely reach your goal. Why can I say this with such conviction? Because this plan has been tried and tested thousands of times and with success. In this respect, I can definitely support the statement: Success can be planned!

This tried and tested three-fold plan includes the components of action, setup, and promotions. But what exactly does this mean? Basically, each of the following subsections is an exact answer to the question of "how."

The first letter A, is for ACTION:
This buzzword speaks for itself. Your goal can be so beautiful and big, so special and personal, but if you don't act, everything else doesn't matter. Your vision becomes worthless. Remember how I made it clear at the beginning that without diligence and work things won't happen? This is true not only in network marketing, but in everything related to do achieving goals in life. In this context, the question of "how" is no longer an issue. Will you, or won't you? No one can take this decision away from you - not even me. That is part of being honest to myself because I don't want to sell you any false promises in this book. When managers, no matter in which industries, or coaches and trainers keep talking about the fact that you can become anything you want and achieve anything you want, they are right. But - there is an essential addition to this and that is: ...within the scope of your current

possibilities. In other words: If you don't want it now, if you say no to the opportunity, then you have also decided, for different path and probably also for another goal. Both decisions are okay, because they are your decisions. However, you should not be surprised that without diligence and hard work that you do not achieve an otherwise achievable goal. Whoever promises otherwise, is neither serious nor honest with you. Nobody has ever become successful on their own and without doing something for it. Through sleeping, being lazy and comfortable, no goal has ever been reached. So, the first component is simply "action" and there is a lot of it in network marketing. This ranges from making appointments, to establishing contacts, to activation. This includes video calls and chats - with the team, with customers, and with contacts who may become future partners. Also important is working with and through messenger services to be and stay in constant contact. Lively communication is crucial to your success in network marketing because our industry thrives on it. That's why we say: Show yourself, come out of your shell and out of your comfort zone. Get off the couch, into life and shine bright for yourself and for others. Whether digital or analog, physical or online. Both ways are ideal, both together optimal.

THE ACTIVE-SLOGAN IS:

**Discover in-person and engage digitally -
or discover digitally and engage in-person!**

How wonderful that there is an extra channel available nowadays besides just physical presence. In our business, it's like winning the lottery but it's only when one is combined with the other. Anyone who primarily searches for, finds and makes contacts on the Internet is still a long way from achieving depth in such a relationship. This can only be achieved through the "live" factor. You certainly know this: Nothing replaces personal contact. Not even a video chat. It is much different when I'm sitting across from a person and can look them in the eye, than when I'm seeing the same person on a monitor. The intensity of this exchange is something completely different. The digital channel is more for volume and freedom in all respects. I can keep in touch with someone anytime and anywhere with various devices via the Internet, both individuals as well as with a group. This makes me independent and is a factor that is harder to implement in real life. It also makes it possible to increase the number of times I communicate with someone. I would barely be able to meet a person two, three or more times a day, let alone a group. But digitally I can - in that respect, this channel stands for independence in any form.

The second letter S, is for SET-UP:
This heading concerns internal business, first and foremost, competence. After all, making, doing and wanting is something wonderful, but in the end, you have to be able to accomplish it. Without the necessary skills to do something correctly and frequently, you will get stuck at least halfway towards your goal, in a swamp of good intentions. This is a frustrating situation that can easily be circumvented: By learning, practicing and gaining experience. Get fit for business and thus ready for your success. Easier said than done? Certainly not, because everything you need is provided in various shapes and sizes - digital and

analog! After all, I don't let my people just go out into the world unprepared. Various training and weekly team meetings will help you. Learn from others and others can learn from you. This is the principle of give and take. I know how important and valuable competence and know-how are but you also have to apply and use them every day, because life experience is unbeatable. Here, too, the rule applies: Just do it! Then it becomes about "learning by doing." Learning does not have the stiff veneer of school. No, because the fun factor is not neglected here either. Training zooms, self-organized team camps, and events hosted by websites from partner companies whet the appetite for more, and mutual exchanges increase self-confidence as well as abilities, skills, and perhaps even the scope of respective goals.

A strong team must not only be built, but also strengthened. "Strength through knowledge" gives you the necessary support. Competence is the surest guide to navigate through all business situations. How can anyone or anything stop you? With action and structure, you are on the straight path to your goal.

The third letter P, is for PROMOTIONS:
It's the famous icing on the cake because after the network comes the marketing. Here it's all about what is recommended. It allows you to ignite the fire in others through motivation. Whether it is special offers, special series, promotions or clearly defined discounts - the easier the access, the more likely a potential customer is to jump over his own shadow to test a product. I know how it is and how skeptical people are. There is an effective tool against this basic skepticism: Promotions! Offer what you have and spark enthusiasm in others. And if you

know how to sell your own story of enthusiasm and success, you're already a winner. Easy access without obstacles - neither in the head nor elsewhere - that's what it's all about. Promotions make it clear that we are first and foremost concerned with people, with their well-being and with helping them and to be clear from the outset away and not to give the impression of bigotry: Of course, this is also a bit of business, no question! Because only turnover generates appropriate income.

But isn't the intention of such a business relevant in the first place? If others are thought of first, and if the resulting by-product is a good source of income, then I call that a decent, ethical, social and super-serious business. Wonderful! And if promotions help one with this valuable and also important mission, then all the better.

In my eyes, the three pillars of the ASP plan are a real treasure trove of success. Why? Because they are crucial for your "how to." There is no compulsion, no "you must", but it is only about what you choose to take from this treasure chest. For these clever promotions give you the chance to shape your path according to your abilities and your strengths. Take what you need, what works best for you and what you feel confident in using and leave everything else behind. You don't need to use tools that are not useful to you in achieving your goals or that you are not comfortable with. Focus on your strengths and use the necessary tools. They are all available to you in this treasure chest. In addition, fun is also on the agenda - and everything that is fun is done gladly and often and with passion. This is the best way to become a great "net-worker."

Do you notice how these three pillars in the plan are linked? How each one is connected and cannot really exist without the other? It highlights that both the system and, above all, the team, are working. We share our knowledge in the team, because this is also a piece of "leadership" and a deep-pink attribute. Therefore, the common English word "beautiful" should really be written with a "p", so that it instead reads: "Pink is **p**eautiful!"

**USE ALL TOOLS
IN THE TREASURE OF
SUCCESS
TO
" WORK NICELY!"**

8th Key: **PASSION**

In the preface I have already described in detail what is meant by the word passion, what triggers it, how it manifests itself and that this state is a desirable automatism. So why does one no longer think anymore, but simply acts based on an inner drive that is almost magical, hardly explainable? The answer is as simple as it is almost sobering: Because it's fun! Because it brings us pleasure! Because it brings a very special satisfaction. The remarkable thing about however, it is that one may only recognize and learn to enjoy the activity over time.

I'll give you an example. Telling other people, wherever you go and wherever you are, about your own business or telling them about it online is a basic task in network marketing. Recommending this business to others, making the many benefits obvious and thus offer them the chance to finally become free and turn their dreams into reality, that is networker duty! Because as you know, you can only grow in this business by helping others to grow even though it's also a well-known fact that this task is not always popular. Some partners feel uncomfortable approaching other people or contacting them via social media or avoid it because they are afraid of the reaction or even rejection. All of this is understandable, because not everyone is born with the ability to approach other people with an outgoing mindset and friendly smile, or who can find the right words during their first online contact. But it should still be done, it's part of the necessary work and job description in network marketing. It is the foundation for activity and a basic requirement to become successful in this business. In a nutshell: Others need to know about you and your business!

In the beginning, you are still far away from passion but the way there is shorter and easier than you might think because "Practice makes perfect!" That's only possible though, by getting out of your own way, fighting your inner demons, and just getting out there. I know I promised you the answer to the "how" question in this book and I intend to keep that promise.

First, I advise you to prepare yourself with a sentence or a very short speech. With words that you normally use. Remember: Authenticity is required! If you "recite" something that sounds foreign and like you've memorized it, you won't get much encouragement. If someone - perhaps your upline - provides you with such an approach, then this is a valuable help because it appears to work for them and is thus tried and tested. But: Use your words, your language. There is also a second thing you should master: Appropriate answers! Also called "objection handling" in network jargon. You can be sure of this: If someone responds to your offer with a negative answer or a "but...", it will always be the same sentences and phrases. A maximum of ten. Mankind is not so spontaneous and creative that it can always and unexpectedly come up with new excuses. This knowledge should make you feel a bit more confident and if you have the right responses ready, if you counter verbally, charmingly, and eloquently, then you've usually won. Simply learn the ten "in case of an emergency" phrases intensively and you'll be ready for the real thing! That's a promise! Okay, so that's one way to get out of your own way - do what needs to be done.

But what does this have to do with passion? A lot! Because by doing and practicing - "training on the job" - you gain increasing confidence. From this security, you generate routine and put aside your initial shyness. Both the routine and the frequent active implementation of your sponsoring activities become second nature to you. Your team grows, and so do your sales. Again, and again, you may encounter people who have the potential to shine in your business, but require some refining and polishing to fully discover their potential. You realize what an unbelievable number of perceptible, even countable advantages it brings you to be active now and to have once prepared yourself intensively. Suddenly, the completion of this task begins to be fun for you despite not being enthusiastic about it in the beginning. Mastering the subject matter, regularly acting, feeling secure, achieving a sense of routine, and finding joy in the work inevitably lead to passion. You do something without thinking too much about why you're doing it. You just do it - because it gives you joy, you know about the benefits and it doesn't require any effort!

There is a reason why I put passion at the end of the Keys to the Secret of Unlimited Success in Network Marketing. This is because it is the ultimate key in the Pink:Code. It is the ultimate achievement, the highest level, and the most intense degree of the Pink:Code. All other keys and their application inevitably lead to a greater or lesser degree to passion. If you have the first seven keys in your hand and open the corresponding seven gates in the code, then you will stand in front of the final lock that has to be opened. It is the "passion" lock and now you are in possession of all the secrets of the Pink:Code.

Everything you do from now on, you do all by yourself with joyful passion because if you automatically do something properly, then it doesn't weigh you down. Everything that we like to do and everything that we know will benefit us to the greatest extent, we do with commitment, with joy and as often as possible. This stage of productivity is the pinnacle of positive emotion, and there's no greater level of motivation possible, making it a true guarantee for success. You have done it: You have deciphered the Pink:Code for yourself and absorbed all of its valuable secrets and associated virtues. Unlimited success in network marketing? Nothing can stand in your way now with all that you have learned and gained from this book. Thanks to the Pink:Code. How do I know this and why can I promise you this success? Because that's exactly what I did and still do. If I can and could do it, then you can do it more exceptionally. That's because you already know so much more and are better equipped with the knowledge required to boost yourself to success. My many experiences over the past years have proven to me and all my great team partners that our path is the right one: Every day with a lot of pink, with a lot of the Pink:Code and above all with intense passion!

THE TWO MOST IMPORTANT FEATURES, THAT DEFINE THE KEY: **PASSION**

1. COMMITMENT TO YOURSELF

Nobody likes to make mistakes and it is even more unpleasant for most people to admit to these mistakes. What a pity as there is nothing better than this. Mistakes have real advantages, are valuable and important and carry an extremely positive message and essence! You are probably surprised about this statement, right? A big question mark now hovers over your head. I can almost see it! And you're now asking yourself, "What's so great about making mistakes?" Well, I can tell you: The learning effect associated with it, because we humans learn more from them than anything else. This is however, under one condition: Making the mistake once and once only. This associated experience brings us forward, helps us with our valuable personality development and is available to us like a good advisor from past experiences throughout life. We continue to build on our knowledge based on our mistakes, develop our character, our abilities, and skills. It is a pity that in modern day society there is the complete opposite culture when it comes to accepting mistakes. To the outside world, alleged perfectionism is always feigned. The media and advertising act as if there are almost only ideal people who can do everything, who achieve everything, who all study with ease, who all have a top job and who are all happy, beautiful, satisfied, wealthy and just somehow perfect! Mistakes do not occur in this illusory world view and certainly not flaws. But all of this has nothing whatsoever to do with reality. Nevertheless, this mindset is more or less drilled into all of us and what is the result? More and more people unfortunately feel that they cannot keep up with this unattainable societal ideal. However, in order not to end up looking like a loser or even a failure, or out of fear of losing connection and thus also affection, approval and prestige, many people deceive themselves and thus also the others in their environment. They lose connection to reality. You certainly know people like that. Those who like to talk big, who act as if they are the greatest, but behind their facade their world looks quite different: Mostly small, gray, and dull. These people live in a make-believe world, are good actors, and wear masks. They want to cover up their mistakes, their alleged shortcomings with a false image of themselves. What a pity - because in this way they stand in the way of their own personality development, because they do not admit their mistakes to themselves, but rather defend them or praise them as "good deeds." With this self-deception however, they unfortunately prevent that they gain insights, experiences, and lessons from exactly these mistakes. All show and no substance! One merely plays a role also because others have a certain expectation of you that you cannot or simply do not want to meet in reality. The Greek poet Aesop wrote a more than fitting fable that sums it up well and who knows, maybe this has also happened to you:

A mouse and a sparrow were sitting under a vine one autumn evening chatting with each other. Suddenly the sparrow chirped to his friend, "Hide, the fox is coming," and quickly flew up into the foliage.

The fox crept up to the vine, his eyes looking longingly at the bunch of overripe grapes. Then he propped himself against the trunk with his front paws, vigorously stretched his body upwards and tried to grab a few grapes with his mouth. But they were hanging too high. Somewhat annoyed, he tried his luck again. This time he made a mighty leap, but again he only snapped at nothing. He tried a third time and jumped with all his might. Full of greed, he reached for the luscious grapes, stretching so far that he tumbled backward onto his back. Not a single leaf had rustled.

The sparrow, who had watched in silence, could no longer contain himself and chirped in amusement, "Mr. Fox, you're aiming too high!" The mouse peeked out from its hiding place and cheekily chirped, "Don't bother, you'll never get the grapes." And like an arrow it shot back into its hole.

The fox gritted his teeth, scrunched up his nose and said haughtily, "They're not ripe enough for me, I don't like sour grapes." With his head held high, he strutted back into the forest...

Welcome to the world of illusions! We all have a self-image of ourselves which is how we wish to be seen or perceived by others. Maybe you see yourself as a helpful person, as someone who is determined or who was born to have a successful career. You are also probably very convinced that you not only belong to this group, but that you live up to this standard and resemble it. This is certainly true in many cases, however, there are also cases in which people are not really the way they would like to be. It consists of developing an identity that one thinks is particularly desirable. Over time though, one believes that this self-image actually corresponds to one's own reality.

The remarkable thing, is that when it comes to other people who are deluding themselves, it is very easy to recognize self-deception - and you have probably experienced it yourself. But what about you? Are you just as easily able to recognize it in yourself? Unfortunately, the probability that you will succeed in doing so on the first attempt is very low because self-deception can only work really well if the deception is simultaneously covered up. Otherwise, we would realize that there is a big difference between what we believe about ourselves and what we actually do. Our consciousness cannot tolerate such a discrepancy and it is one of the most important tasks of our psyche to establish and maintain a coherent world view. Conscious self-deception would not be compatible with that - that would lead to a number of contradictions within us.

The question is how you can get to know yourself and the answer is, only through brutal honesty towards yourself.

1. Write down a list of ten character traits that you believe apply to yourself. Describe your personality and keep going until you have listed all ten of these traits.

2. Now write down when and where you consciously acted against yourself and your character. Example: You consider yourself a very punctual person but when did you last arrive late and why? You think you are neat and tidy, but when and where did you notice yourself creating a mess? On the desk? In the kitchen? Were you unprepared for a meeting?

3. When and where were you last dishonest with others, especially with your team? Did you deceive them or did your actions not match your words?

Self-questioning is so important because in passion, it's about giving yourself more than just a promise. One that you must keep, and not skirt around with excuses. It's more than a promise - it's a commitment to yourself. Think of it as a valid contract with yourself. One that you must keep and fulfill. This commitment, this "contract with yourself" is the positive and at the same time written awareness of your real, most intimate, and individual goals and visions! However, this contract also reminds you that if you honor it and fulfill it, you will attain your goals.

PINK:CODE

Isn't that amazing? You only have to be able to rely on yourself. But let's be honest: Who can you rely on more than yourself? You are loyal to yourself and have faith in your personality and in the Pink:Code, along with its eight keys.

A few chapters ago I already made it clear to you that a commitment has a considerably higher value than a promise. It entails much more and therefore it is just as necessary that you know about yourself beforehand and that you are not just someone who deceives themselves and pretends. From now on, you don't know how to pretend. It's time to look behind your own facade now, recognize yourself, reset and start again. Then, and really only then, can the commitment work.

This commitment to yourself is best written down or printed out! Hang it up in a very prominent place, not in the closet, but where you can see it all the time - and others too. This way you will be constantly reminded of your own commitment to yourself, and you will have to explain to others what that commitment is all about. This is important because you are widening the "commitment radius" even more and will have to explain to others what this commitment is about. In this way, your commitment makes you more or less liable to yourself and ensures that you stay on track, pursue your goals tenaciously and with joy, and in the process make the pink status shine even brighter and stronger!

2. THE PINNACLE: LEVEL OF PASSION

There is hardly anything more magical and captivating than enthusiasm and dedication. We often admire others for it and show them great respect. You certainly know this when you tip your imaginary hat to someone else because you admire their performance and what they have achieved so far. You become a fan. That's all well and good, but what do your fans actually do? Who is tipping their hat to you? Where is your performance that others cheer about? I bet you're at least on your way there. Now that you know the secrets to boundless success in network marketing, and especially now that you know how to do it, what do you have to do? You already have the eight valuable keys of the Pink:Code in your hands and all you have to do is use them. So that's why I also want to encourage you to always make one fan happy and satisfied: Yourself! Be your best and biggest fan! Then, others will follow you. Be the hero of your own story.

Because we all love heroes - always have, always will. The history books are full of heroes. Why? Because these people always burn with passion for a cause, they stand firm for something and never let themselves be swayed. That is why respect is paid to a hero. It is one characteristic that unites all successful people - and now, with the Pink:Code, you belong to these people too: That is passion. It lets you persevere when setbacks or critics come. Passion outlasts short-term enthusiasm. It makes our eyes sparkle when we talk about our ideas or successes and this passion in turn infects people who see and hear it. Often, passion is the deciding factor in whether we are heading for fortune or fiasco. This passion is your personal promise of happiness. Namely, your promise to yourself that no one but you is responsible for fulfilling your own wishes, making your own dreams come true and turning your own visions into reality. If not you, then who? Only you can do that - with your newfound passion.

With your passion and all the keys of the Pink:Code, you have incredible potential because this newly acquired passion for something really releases undreamt of forces within you. Passion is what distinguishes those who are successful from those who aren't. But you possess it! However, that's not the end of the story. Passion and determination are also necessary. The great US talk show host and author Oprah Winfrey, once said it remarkably in a quote: "Passion is energy. Feel the power that comes from focusing on what excites you."

Anyone who has passion for something also has the will. But not everyone with the will also has passion. This includes this unique energy that literally emanates out of a person with passion from the inside. The Pink:Code gives you access to it, lets you get to the source of this passion energy and draw from it. You are breaking boundaries. It is not only your enthusiasm that drives you, but a special energetic form of ambition that is active in your heart, mind, body, and soul and that makes you accomplish things that are almost beyond human. Your inner self in turn gives you the greatest feeling of happiness possible. All this manifests itself in passion. You don't even feel the drawbacks anymore because you do everything with passion - without ifs and buts. You reach your goal without conditions. Successful people who have reached this stage don't have to be particularly talented, they are not exceptional and they are not blessed with super-powers at birth. They have all just reached the next level. The pinnacle of purposeful activity. With unconditional dedication to their actions, with complete application of the Pink values and the virtues associated with them. Because in this dimension they have realized: passion overcomes all obstacles. Passion is thus the highest level of one's own actions.

But if one's own passion is already pinnacle of emotions, then there is still a crowning achievement. The famous cherry or the icing on the cake: To awaken passion in others. Nothing else can top that because this is a truly noble task, especially in network marketing. It is the absolute top management task. Encouraging others in this way to bring out the best in you not only gives you deep satisfaction but it also spurs you on. It won't make things easier, but there are a few good pointers as to what sustains business people's enthusiasm and ignites their passion:

1. Purpose:
Who would want to do work for things or goals that are not really important or do not play a sustainable role? One would engage in meaningless activities because the feeling of being just an insignificant, small cog in the big wheel paralyzes any eagerness to work in the long run and suffocates any desire. Everyone wants to know that their work creates added value, that it is important and even indispensable in a certain way. If you convey exactly that to your partners, you will awaken their enthusiasm anew.

2. Recognition:
Money is right and important! Fair, appropriate pay is even more so. But money never compensates for a lack of recognition. No matter what you create or achieve - you want others to recognize your good performance. Praise is a form of attention, an extremely positive one. High performers can and should never get enough of it. Therefore: If you praise a lot, you become a role model for others.

3. Growth:
The phrase "lifelong learning" always sounds like a challenge, but it's

in our own best interest: We all want to develop further, grow in our jobs, acquire more responsibility and creative freedom, and make a career for ourselves. However, only where people can do this can their passion flourish. Anything else would be a real motivation killer.

4. Autonomy:
Freedom and self-determination are huge driving forces. In fact, they are often one of the most decisive reasons why people choose the network marketing business. Therefore: Show others how they can become more independent - and you will awaken pure passion in them!

Passion with a maximum degree of intensity. I wholeheartedly wish this for you. However, you should never forget that honesty and the Pink:Code demand: Before fame, there is always sweat. The Pink:Code will actively support you to turn your sweat into your success. Last but not least, live and experience your passion every day. In the end, it is the perfect and ideal way to grasp the meaning of life by living and experiencing your passion daily. This is your promise - first to yourself and then to your team with all its great talents. Virtues and qualities that shine in pink and that are the resounding proof that it works and is almost a blessing for everyone:

The Pink:Code!

A word of thanks, dear readers...

The Pink:Code is not an obligation- it's a choice! Not a "must", but a "can." Its contents have more than helped me. They have made me what I am today: A happy, successful and above all fulfilled woman, a networker who can enjoy indescribable freedom. And that's exactly why I wanted to share this happiness with you. With this book I wanted to give you an insight into my life, but also into the workings of our successful team. It should be a colorful, rich buffet for you that is full of valuable ingredients and from which you can take what you want and what you need.

My wish for you: Find the personal path to your passion. And if my Pink:Code can help you - even better. It would make me incredibly happy. I know: You have wonderful strengths, and you might even discover some additional ones in yourself. Especially if you are always honest with yourself. From my whole Pink heart, I wish you success in finding your way and that you stay committed to it. And I wish you many people who will accompany you and believe in you as much as mine have. Something for which I am infinitely grateful.

You and the experiences from my personal Pink:Code have carried me through the waves of life. But that swell is part of it, it makes for an intense life. If there are people by your side who give you the necessary peace, who support you, who help you to get up, who celebrate great victories with you and who are also a constant in your life when things get difficult, then gratitude is a motivating emotion. That's exactly what I wish for you too because I get to experience this gratitude every day. Not only for of that but also because of the insights and perceptions that I recognized and experienced as my Pink:Code.

And because of that, I would like to explicitly thank my family for ever-

ything they have done for me. First and foremost, my parents, who have given me so much on my journey through life, from whom I have been able to learn so much and who have exemplified and thus given me and passed on such important values and virtues. Through them I know how much you can get ahead with kindness, diligence and a portion of carefreeness and what it means to put other people in the center of your own life. Thank you for that!

A huge thank you of course goes to my amazing husband, who has always supported me with all his energy, always had my back and was - and is - always there for me! That means everything to me! The same goes for all my friends and of course for my sensational team, whom I can never thank enough. And there is one more person I would like to mention: That is all those people who didn't believe in the system. You all motivated me twice over and at the same time proved to me that one must never lose faith in themselves. Because this belief is the force that ultimately leads you to your goal - to your personal Pink:Code that results in your own passion. Thanks to all of you!

Your

Stefanie

**ONLY ONE PERSON
IS REQUIRED,
TO BE RESPONSIBLE
FOR THE CHANGE
IN THE LIVES OF
THOUSANDS OF PEOPLE.**

**BE AWARE
OF THIS VALUABLE
LIFE-CHANGING MISSION.**

**YOU HOLD
THE CODE FOR ITS
IMPLEMENTATION
IN YOUR HANDS!**

PROVIDING SERVICE TO *Many* LEADS TO TRUE GREATNESS.

ENJOY YOUR JOURNEY TO *Success*

THINK PINK.
DREAM BIG.
WORK HARD.
DRINK PINK.

Note TO SELF!

Note TO SELF!

Note TO SELF!

Note TO SELF!

Milton Keynes UK
Ingram Content Group UK Ltd.
UKHW051048021223
433483UK00021B/1210